PERFECT WORLD, REAL WORLD

The Secret Weapon for Achieving Financial Independence

Published by MONEY-PORTAL
© 2023 Jacob Nayman
All rights reserved.

The knowledge and practices in this book are rooted in Nayman's extensive experience, distilling more than 25 years of expertise in his role as a leading investment advisor to the world's wealthiest.

The holy grail of this book is to achieve two key goals.

Goal one:

Increase your wealth and become financially independent.

Goal two:

No longer be manipulated by other people or entities.

To achieve these key goals:

You will learn the strategies of the secret weapon.

As a result of rapid economic and technological changes, the middle class becomes smaller and smaller each year. The result of this global phenomenon is that in the future, the world will be divided into two groups of people:

the rich and established –
and everyone else.

Here's the truth: as the years go by,
if you aren't part of the first group,
you'll be part of the second.

Fortunately, there's no predestination.

You *can* become rich and established
by employing the strategies of the secret weapon
for building your wealth.

The knowledge and strategies outlined in this book are based on Nayman's extensive knowledge and experience gained over 25 years in his role as a leading investment and economic advisor to the world's wealthiest.

Infusing your life with the secret weapon will enable you to achieve the most important goal of the 21st century:

FINANCIAL INDEPENDENCE

Contents

Part Two: Promoting Social Issues

Introduction

We live in a world that's overloaded with manipulated information. Each year, powerful people and entities spend billions of dollars to data mine our habits and lifestyles, then use that data to shape and control our minds, decisions, and eventually, our lives. Their main motive? To impose on us the economic goals and desires of the world's most powerful.

While publicly wielding a philanthropic agenda that purports to care about *us*, their clandestine agenda proves that they see us only as a means to an end: a pawn, an object that serves *their* desires and goals – often at the expense of *our* aims and ambitions.

In this manipulative environment, we fall victim to the illusion that our decisions and actions stem from our free will. Most often, however, our decisions and actions are informed by manipulated information and fake news that was intentionally created by the world's most powerful and sophisticated people and entities.

Cutting through the confusion of this challenging environment, *Perfect World, Real World* will give you the knowledge and tools you need – including the secret weapon – to help you achieve financial independence based on your personal desires, values, and goals. Once you know the secret weapon, you will no longer be tempted to let other people or entities control your mind and influence your decisions.

Throughout my 25 years of experience as an economic advisor to the top one percent, I interacted with thousands of the world's most rich and powerful – people with great minds, and from all walks of life – and every one of them with a different personality and set of values. What I learned during those years was that their ability to solve problems, meet challenges, and attain goals was consistent with elements they used successfully, over and over again. What they all have in common is that they were not only financially independent, but intellectually autonomous as well.

Based on the wisdom and experience of those successful and powerful people, I adopted the generic elements that proved their effectiveness and created the secret weapon.

Over the last decade as an economic advisor to senior executives, I have employed the secret weapon – and the successes have been resounding.

From the start, people who applied the secret weapon have shared that it helped them tremendously, not only in their professional lives, but in their own personal lives too. After witnessing firsthand, the positive impact of the secret weapon on people's lives, I decided to write this book to help millions of others improve their lives by using the secret weapon.

The building of the secret weapon was based on the synergy of many masterful minds. The power of the secret weapon can be expressed by a quote from Sir Isaac Newton in 1675: "If I have seen further, it is by standing on the shoulders of giants." The strategies of the secret weapon integrate the experience and wisdom of thousands of great minds.

Infusing your life with the secret weapon will enable you to achieve the most important goal in the 21st century:

FINANCIAL
INDEPENDENCE

Yours,

Jacob Nayman

Part One:

Financial Independence

Chapter 1

Making the Impossible Possible

What we need to achieve big goals

To achieve big, challenging goals, you don't need innate charisma, leadership abilities, brilliant powers of the mind, or a Harvard MBA. As we will demonstrate, by using strategies of the secret weapon, you can achieve your desired goals – even without those qualifications.

The crowning achievement

An investment company that manages over 100 billion dollars gives a presentation to their elite customers, proudly showcasing their phenomenal ability to make successful investments for their clients.

Mid-presentation, they share their crowning achievement.

They present an investment that they made three

years ago. The initial investment was 500 million dollars and now, after only three years, it's worth close to two billion dollars.

At this stage, you are likely thinking that this successful company can afford to hire the best professionals and most brilliant minds in the field of economics and investments. They've likely hired exceptional graduates of Wharton or the Harvard Business School, or have otherwise assembled a brilliant, sophisticated team to achieve this impressive result.

But as you will soon see, any person with ambition and a sound mind can achieve this investment result – simply by using the strategies of the secret weapon.

So, what happened three years ago?

Let's begin.

The investment company's private clandestine agenda

Goal

To buy from the grape growers their entire industry for a price that's only one-third of its real value.

Problem

The grape growers only trust those from their industry, not outsiders.

Solution

Approach a grape grower who is trusted and respected by his colleagues and offer him a large incentive to persuade his fellow growers to sell their assets at a very low price.

The "trusted" grape grower's large incentive

We will buy your assets, which today are worth two million dollars, and pay you eight million dollars. You will receive the extra six million dollars on your assets only if you will persuade your fellow grape growers to sell their assets, worth an aggregate $1.5 billion, at the very low price of $500 million.

The public agenda

Build the problem

A key strategy of the secret weapon is that the problem will be fully tailored to correspond with the provided solution.

In the preparation stage – *before* the presentation – we decide on the desired solution. From there, we develop the problem. Then, in the presentation stage, we present the problem first, and finally the solution.

BE PREPARED
We know in advance our desired solution. So, we craft the problem based on the solution. This creates a kind of magic — when we present the solution, it seems perfect. Uncoincidentally, it's fully suited to the problem.

The presentation to the grape growers

The trusted grape grower will be the one to present the public agenda. To his colleagues, who trust him, he will illustrate the tailored problem and provide the solution.

The problem — fully tailored to the solution

The trusted grape grower (for getting his extra six million dollars on his assets) – will say to his

19

fellow grape growers: In every day that passes, we, the grape growers, lose a lot of money because we are divided and in competition with one another. This means our prices are low and our profits are meager.

The solution

Now we have the opportunity of a lifetime – a game changer – a chance to change this reality: there is a prestigious investment company that is willing to buy our assets for a good price. If we do this, we can charge a lot more for our product because we will not be competing among ourselves. Of course, after the sale, our assets will legally belong to the investment company, but as part of the deal, we will continue to enjoy a percentage of the sales.

BE AWARE!
The trusted grape grower, who had a big incentive of six million dollars, persuaded his colleagues to sell their assets without their awareness that they received only one-third of the value of their assets.

The main principle of an effective public agenda

The public agenda will be crafted based on the "music" that will create the biggest impact on people's motivation to take action.

In retrospect

The grape growers could have been more cautious. If they wouldn't have automatically trusted their fellow member and the company, they could have invested a few thousand dollars for an outside expert to professionally assess the real value of their assets, and it's likely that if they had done it, the deal would not have gone through.

Note

All the examples in this book including this one, are based on true stories. Some details have been changed to protect privacy.

The Main Points

One of the key strategies of the secret weapon

We know in advance our desired solution. So, we craft the problem based on the solution. This creates a kind of magic — when we present the solution, it seems perfect. Uncoincidentally, it's fully suited to the problem.

What we need to achieve big goals

Any person with ambition and a sound mind who uses the secret weapon strategies can achieve big, challenging goals — even without innate charisma, leadership abilities, a brilliant mind, or a Harvard MBA.

Chapter 2

Manipulation

The easy way to succeed

When Julius Caesar achieved his victory, he famously said, "Veni, vidi, vici" – "I came, I saw, I conquered." In Caesar's days, the first century BCE, the leading method for achieving desires and goals was through the power of the sword. In the 21st century, however, the power of the sword has been replaced by the weapon of manipulation.

What is manipulation?

Manipulation is the use of unfair means of deception to influence, exploit, and control people's minds and, eventually, actions. A manipulator's main goal is to achieve their clandestine desires and goals, even at the expense of others. Manipulation gives the manipulated person a false sense that they are acting of their own free will. They are unaware that they are victims of manipulation.

Why manipulation is the weapon of choice

When individuals or entities use illegal means to force their desires and goals on others, their actions violate criminal law. As a result, those individuals or entities will be subject to punishment and sanctions under the law. Conversely, using manipulation in place of force offers three key advantages for the manipulators.

First, manipulation is very effective. It creates quick results in a short time frame. And in certain circumstances, it can even be considered legitimate – especially in the business world.

Second, it is difficult to legally prove use of manipulation because one has to show that the manipulation was committed with an intentional motive and a deliberate act.

Third, in the rare cases when the act of manipulation is supported with sufficient evidence, it's not often considered a criminal action that violates the law. This means it will not lead to punishment. In most instances when people or entities practice manipulation, they will get the same results as practicing illegal means of force, but without punishment or sanctions.

The guy with the Ferrari

A man meets a woman, and for their first date, he arrives on the scene in a Ferrari. Sporting a genuine Rolex and accompanied by a giant bodyguard, he invites his new love interest to a romantic dinner on his private yacht. He informs the woman that his last name is connected to that of a very rich and famous family of billionaires. The woman's initial impression of the man is that he's very wealthy. For their second date, he invites her to fly with him in his private jet to a restaurant in Paris. At this stage, the woman is fully convinced that he is affluent and well established.

After several weeks of romantic interactions, the woman feels a deep mental and emotional connection with the man. It's at this time that he kindly says to her, "I have a temporary cash problem. Please help me." Then, acting of her own free will, without any force or threat, the woman transfers her life savings – $700K – to his bank account. She also wrongly assumes that because she perceives him as wealthy, that the risk she takes by giving him her life savings is inconsequential – or worse, that there is no risk at all.

Time passes and she still hasn't been reimbursed. She has a big problem. Why? Because it was her choice to transfer the money to the Ferrari guy. He, of course, would have said, "I will give you the money back."

BE AWARE!

In most countries, when she approaches the police to report the man, they will tell her that they cannot help her because his actions are not considered criminal; they will say that it's a matter of civil conflict.

In this case, we see how, through immoral manipulation without any threat of violence or force, the Ferrari guy took the woman's life savings – all while escaping punishment.

Mission Impossible

Imagine you work as a high-profile lobbyist and are hired by a large cybersecurity firm.

Your mission:

Get the cybersecurity firm a full exemption from paying billions of tax dollars each year.

If you succeed in your mission, according to the contract you signed with the cybersecurity firm, they will transfer a commission of five million dollars to your bank account.

Let's begin.

First line of action

You go to the department of commerce in your country and ask their officials for a full tax exemption for the big cybersecurity company you represent. Their immediate response to your request will be no. Why? They explain to you that if they exempt the cybersecurity company you represent from paying taxes, then every other business in the country will ask to enjoy the same privilege. This, of course, would create a very big problem for the department and country: exemptions for all companies would result in no taxes being paid at all.

BE AWARE!
Now you understand that you must approach the mission with a different line of action.

You ask yourself:

What can I do differently to achieve the mission and get the five-million-dollar commission?

To succeed in the mission, you apply elements of the secret weapon. You define the problem differently. You understand that your request represents, at its core, a social problem that you have to address. The social problem is why your cybersecurity company should get a tax exemption of billions of dollars while other companies must continue to pay full taxes. Therefore, you have to find a mechanism that will give a social justification for the full tax exemption.

Challenge accepted

You concentrate your efforts on building a public agenda in which you logically explain why exempting your cybersecurity company from paying taxes will make the world a better place from the standpoint of the government. You must also craft a powerful justification that legitimizes the government's decision to exempt only your cybersecurity company from paying taxes, while other businesses continue to pay in full.

Second line of action

You arrange a second meeting with the commerce department officials. When you meet with them, your opening sentence will be:

I come to you with a unique and effective solution to a big, important social problem.

The public agenda:

The big problem

Our country doesn't have enough high-quality, well-paying jobs for our workers. The main reason is that we don't have the right economic conditions and incentives to attract wealthy international companies to our country.

The unique, effective solution that will make our country a better place to live in

I come to you to suggest an important regulation that will encourage large international companies to invest in our country. This new regulation will produce a lot of high-quality, well-paying jobs – jobs that our citizens need.

To carry out this important task, we must offer those international companies a compelling incentive: full tax exemption. Then they will move their location and come to our country, bringing us quality, high-paying jobs.

Of course, there are objective criteria that I suggest you use to give these companies their tax exemptions:

- They should be an international company with headquarters in our country.
- The company should be large, with over 300,000 workers worldwide.
- The company should be publicly worth more than 300 billion dollars.

And guess what: unsurprisingly, only your cybersecurity company meets these three criteria. These criteria give your company a uniqueness that justifies their tax exemption – while other companies must still pay full taxes.

And now, as a lobbyist who has successfully used the secret weapon, your chances of delivering your agenda and earning the five-million-dollar commission is greater than ever.

But hold on

Until now, we have shown the impact of only the public agenda. For the magic to happen and for you to harness the full support of decision makers and earn the multimillion-dollar commission, we must also introduce the secret clandestine agenda.

The clandestine agenda:

Improve the world of the decision makers by offering large incentives

Government officials know with certainty that if they approve the deal, they personally have a lot to gain. They know that after retiring from their jobs as government officials, they will secure lucrative jobs – ones with multimillion-dollar annual salaries – and major perks in the cybersecurity company for which they procured the tax exemption. The officials know that these perks and staggering salaries will not necessarily reflect their qualifications, but rather their past contribution to the cybersecurity company.

BE AWARE!
The high-profile lobbyist never promised the government officials anything.

How did the officials know with certainty that they personally have a lot to gain if they approve the deal?

Because this has been the common practice (how things are done) for many years in most democratic countries.

This example demonstrates how using elements of the secret weapon can give you powerful strategic tools to enable you to carry out a mission that is seemingly impossible.

To succeed in this challenge of mission impossible, we must deliver the public agenda, while also wielding – in secret – the clandestine agenda.

To harness the decision makers' active support, we first need to give a public justification for why their support for our agenda will improve the country. This justification serves the needs of the government officials to explain why they will exempt the cybersecurity company, and not others, from paying taxes.

The Main Points

Why manipulation is the weapon of choice

First, using the weapon of manipulation is very effective. It can create quick results in a short time frame.

Second, it is very hard to legally prove that manipulation has occurred in the first place.

Third, even when an act of manipulation is proven, it is not usually considered a criminal act that deserves punishment.

Chapter 3

Gain Financial Independence
Three must-have abilities for success

If we look at the middle of the 20th century in America, an average person could finish high school, work at a car factory in a blue-collar job, and raise with honor and prosperity a family with three kids. But in our days, the 21st first century, the cost of living has become staggering. And the ability to earn the sums of money that are needed for managing a reasonable lifestyle and gaining financial independence is more challenging.

How much money do we need?

In order to feel financially secure, most people reply that they need $200,000 a year at least. If you take a couple in their 30s who have two children, it certainly makes sense.

Assuming that the average life expectancy is 80

years, a simple calculation shows that this couple will need an aggregate amount of $10,000,000 in order to maintain a reasonable standard of living over the next 50 years.

BE PREPARED

The practical way to generate additional income is to manage our finances in an optimal manner. We can do this by building a private investment portfolio.

The must-have abilities to achieve financial independence

Ability one: Identify manipulations and say no

The first important element for becoming financially independent is the ability to quickly identify when the weapon of manipulation is being used on us, and to say no.

We live in a reality that supports the illusion that we are surrounded by endless attractive opportunities.

But in fact, people and entities want to harness our scarce resources of time, money, and mental energy to further their agenda. They declare that their main goal is to serve our desires and goals while using the weapon of manipulation to exploit our limited resources and promote their clandestine agenda – which, in most cases, doesn't suit our desires and goals.

When we possess the ability to quickly and effectively identify when the weapon of manipulation is being used on us, then we can say no to their agendas and proactively avoid spending our precious, limited resources on things that don't truly align with our values and desires. Instead, we can use our limited resources of time, money, and mental energy – those that were saved when we said no – to focus on agendas that promote our personal desires, values, and goals.

"The difference between successful people and really successful people is that really successful people say no to almost everything."

– *Warren Buffett*

Ability two: Harness active support for your agenda

The second important element for becoming financially independent is the ability to harness active support for your private agenda.

When we want to promote a big, important agenda – such as raising millions of dollars for a private startup or to advance to a higher managerial position in our workplace or to effectively promote our business's product or service – we need the support of other people or entities.

The secret weapon will enhance this ability tremendously. Using the elements of the secret weapon will give you the ability to harness the scarce resources of time, money, and mental energy to actively – and effectively – promote your private agenda.

Ability three: Build and preserve your wealth

The third ability you have to possess in order to become financially independent is the ability to build and preserve your wealth. The ability to earn money from working alone is not enough. When we have the right tools and knowledge to manage a private investment portfolio that includes stocks, bonds, real estate, and commodities, this creates significant passive income.

BE AWARE!

Most well-established people gained their wealth from their investments, not from their income.

"Never depend on a single income.
Make an investment to create a second source."

— *Warren Buffett*

The Main Points

The three must-have abilities for financial success

The first ability you have to possess in order to become financially independent is the ability to quickly identify when the weapon of manipulation is being used on you, and to say no.

The second ability you have to possess in order to become financially independent is the ability to harness people's limited resources to support your private agenda.

The third ability you have to possess in order to become financially independent is the ability to build and preserve your wealth. The ability to earn money from working alone is not enough.

Chapter 4

Perfect World vs. Real World

What you see is what you get vs. deception

> "Most of economics can be summarized in four words: 'People respond to incentives.' The rest is commentary."

> — *Steven Landsburg*

Incentives are the cornerstone of modern life. They encourage action, and can be economic – or value – oriented. People respond to many different types of incentives, some altruistic, most, not so much. Some are motivated by a sense of duty or community in how they live their lives or the choices that they make. The reality, however, is that the vast majority of people and corporations are driven primarily by financial incentive.

For example, tax incentives can be used as an effective tool to encourage people to save and invest more of their income.

BE AWARE!

Incentives are an important tool to promote agendas. In the perfect world the incentives will be more value-oriented than in the real world.

Perfect World vs. Real World

The Perfect World
Guiding principles:

- People respond to incentives.
- What you see is what you get – the private and public agendas are the same.
- Make the world a better place – social interests will prevail over private interests.
- A dichotomous solution, with only two options drives people to act.

Main Traits

The perfect world is a moral utopian world without manipulations in which people are seen as intelligent entities who deserve fair treatment. It's a world in which what you see is what you get – that is, the private and public agendas are the same. Trust, transparency, and shared goals are used as powerful, effective weapons to achieve a common goal that benefits all involved parties.

The main tool to motivate others to actively support private and public agendas is to connect the values, desires, and goals in the agenda to other people's values, desires, and goals.

BE PREPARED

In the perfect world, when we make a decision to actively support an agenda, we will realize our authentic desires and goals.

The Real World
Guiding principles:

- People respond to incentives.
- Manipulation and deceit – the private and public agendas aren't the same.

- Make your world a better place – private interests will prevail over social interests.
- A dichotomous solution, with only two options drives people to act.

Main Traits

The real world is an immoral world characterized by manipulation and deceit. Entities (people or corporations) see other people in society only as a means to an end: a pawn or object that should be exploited to serve their selfish goals and desires.

These entities champion public and private agendas that are not the same. Their public agenda camouflages the clandestine agenda: it pretends to serve our values and desires and to care about our well-being. But unbeknownst to most of the population, their private agenda doesn't correspond to their public agenda.

The entities use the weapon of manipulation on people to achieve their clandestine agenda that predominantly serves their desires and goals. Even worse, it's most often done at the expense of other people's personal aims and ambitions.

47

If, in this manipulative reality, we're unable to recognize when we are being manipulated, we impair our ability to make decisions that serve our values, desires, and goals.

The type of manipulation that is used to promote an agenda in the real world

When people or entities look to promote their clandestine agenda, they manipulate by camouflaging this private agenda with a presentation of a public agenda that corresponds to people's desires and goals. This kind of manipulation will harness active support from people without their awareness that they actually support the clandestine agenda, which doesn't serve their values, ambitions, and aims.

Eat as much as you desire

In the past, large corporate food companies claimed that the only reason people were suffering from obesity is because they weren't exercising enough. And they published research to prove their claim. What they didn't publicize, however, was that they sponsored the research. They also invested a lot money in advertising, creating commercials to deliver their message: "Eat as much as you desire, exercise, and you will not be obese." This kind of manipulation served their economic agenda at the expense of those who adopted that harmful agenda – and usually remained obese and less healthy in the process.

The Main Points

The perfect world

- What you see is what you get — the private and public agendas are the same.
- Make the world a better place — social interests will prevail over private interests.

The real world

- Manipulation and deceit — the private and public agendas aren't the same.
- Make your world a better place — private interests will prevail over social interests.

Chapter 5

The Secret Weapon

Make *your* world a better place

The secret weapon is equipped with powerful
strategies designed to harness active support for
private and/or public agendas. The secret weapon can
be used in a moral way, like how things are done in
the "perfect moral world" – a utopian world where
what you see is what you get. Conversely, it can be
used effectively in the "real world," which is a world
of manipulation and deceit.

In both the perfect and real worlds, the secret
weapon strategies are effective in delivering their
purpose: harnessing active support for private and

public agendas. The secret weapon strategies can be used for a variety of goals: to gain a higher position in your workplace; to raise money for your startup company; to effectively promote your business's product or service; or to endorse a social agenda that connects to your core values and beliefs.

The flip-flops factory
(Perfect World)

STAGE ONE
Build a private agenda

Goal

Sell many more flip-flops at a high price, while also improving the lives of single mothers and their children.

Problem

This is a highly competitive industry as there are many companies that sell flip-flops.

Solution

The factories where the flip-flops are made will be in Afghanistan, which will offer moral value to those who buy the flip-flops.

Guiding principles for delivering phase one

First guiding principle

Develop an incentive, whether economic – or values – based, to lead decision makers to actively support the goal.

Second guiding principle

Social interests will prevail over private interests.

The secret weapon strategy: Phase one

Provide a significant incentive to decision makers (customers) that is relevant for achieving your goal.

The big incentive to the decision makers

The customers who buy the flip-flops that we produce will support the existence of the flip-flop factories in Afghanistan. The implication is that some of the customer's money will go directly to single mothers in Afghanistan who work in the flip-flop factories. This money will enable those single mothers to raise children who will likely not have an economic incentive to join a terrorist organization.

STAGE TWO
Build a public agenda

Guiding principle for delivering phase two

Transparency: what you see is what you get.

The secret weapon strategy: Phase two

Exploit a big, real problem that exists in society. The problem will be fully tailored to correspond with the provided solution. The tailored problem will present the given solution as unique, and as having a large, positive societal impact.

A big problem — fully tailored to the solution

The main reason that children join terrorist groups in Afghanistan is because they are being raised in poor families. Most of these children come from single-mother families who cannot economically support them. Therefore, there is a high probability that their children will join terrorist groups who give them money.

Guiding principle for delivering phase three

Effectiveness logically convinces people that the solution has a high probability of materializing.

The secret weapon strategy: Phase three

Explain in a logical way (cause and effect) why the solution is effective in solving the problem.

Why the solution is effective in solving the problem

The main reason that children join terrorist organizations is not ideological; it comes as a result of living in very poor families, most of them managed by single mothers. If the single mother has a secure job in a flip-flop factory, she could provide for the economic needs of her children. In turn, the children will not have an economic incentive to join terrorist groups.

Guiding principle for delivering phase four

Every solution, even an effective one, can create or be perceived as creating a new problem. Therefore, we must prepare a justification in advance. We must show that the added value of implementing the solution is greater than any possible problems.

The secret weapon strategy: Phase four

Legitimize the agenda. Present the given solution as socially justified: a solution that makes the world a better place.

Why the solution is socially justified

The solution will not only solve the single mother's problem, it will also make the world a better place because fewer children will become terrorists. This also means that there will be fewer future victims of terrorist acts.

Guiding principle for delivering phase five

A dichotomous choice of only two options impacts people's lizard mind and leads them to act.

Lizard Brain

The lizard brain is the most primitive part of the brain; the brain stem. It is the part of a person's psyche or personality dominated by instinct or impulse rather than rational thought.

The secret weapon strategy: Phase five

Build a call to action that is based on a dichotomy. Present a solution with only two options, where one option is good and the other is bad.

Call to action

If single mothers have steady jobs with sufficient income, there is a high probability that their children will become normative citizens. But, if these children continue to live in poor families, it is likely that, in the end, they will join a terrorist group. In any case, the customer has already decided to buy flip-flops: if they buy them from us, they win twice.

STAGE THREE
Harness active support

Present the solution from the agenda as effective, socially justified, and as a unique approach that solves a big, important problem. In the end, call for action.

Become a new senator (The Real World)

STAGE ONE
Build a private agenda

Goal

Become a new senator.

Problem

To win the election and become a senator, the candidate needs 200 million dollars.

Solution

Campaign for a big tax cut for the rich.

Guiding principles for delivering phase one

First guiding principle

Provide a big incentive, whether values-based or economic, to lead decision makers to actively support the goal.

Second guiding principle

Private interests will prevail over social interests.

The secret weapon strategy: Phase one

Provide a significant incentive to decision makers that is relevant for achieving your goal.

The clandestine agenda

During the candidate's campaign to become a senator, their main platform will be that the government must substantially cut taxes for the rich. In return, the rich will be highly incentivized to contribute 200 million dollars to their campaign.

STAGE TWO
Build a public agenda

Guiding principle for delivering phase two

Manipulation: camouflage the clandestine agenda. (Cut tax for the rich and in return get the 200 million dollars needed to win the election.)

The secret weapon strategy: Phase two

Exploit a big, real problem that exists in society. The problem will be fully tailored to correspond with the provided solution. The tailored problem will present the given solution as unique, and as having a large, positive impact on society.

BE AWARE!

Uniqueness can explain why the given solution is a better choice than other solutions. Big impacts grab people's attention and influence their emotions.

A big problem — fully tailored to the solution

Today's high unemployment rate is harmful to the poor and middle class. The main reason for the burgeoning unemployment rate is that the rich are paying taxes that are too high. Because of the high tax rate, they don't have enough available money to invest in creating more jobs.

Guiding principle for delivering phase three

Effectiveness persuades people that the solution has a high probability of materializing.

The secret weapon strategy: Phase three

Explain in a logical way (cause and effect) why the solution is effective in solving the problem.

Why the solution is effective in solving the problem

If the government makes considerable tax cuts to the revenues of the rich, then society's wealthiest will have more available money to invest in expanding existing businesses or creating new ones. Decreasing taxes for the rich will result in more jobs for the poor and middle class.

Guiding principle for delivering phase four

Every solution, even an effective one, can create or be perceived as creating a new problem. Therefore, we must prepare a justification in advance.

BE PREPARED
If the solution has the potential to create problems (real or perceived), we must show that the added value of implementing the solution is greater than any possible problems.

The secret weapon strategy: Phase four

Legitimize the clandestine agenda. Present the given solution as socially justified – a solution that makes the world a better place.

Why the solution is socially justified

Lowering taxes for the rich will not harm the poor or middle class because more jobs mean more tax for the government. This will offset the loss of taxes from the rich.

Guiding principle for delivering phase five

A dichotomous choice of only two options impacts people's lizard mind and leads them to take action.

The secret weapon strategy: Phase five

B uild a call to action that is based on a dichotomy. Present a solution with only two options, where one option is good and the other is bad.

Call to action

G iven that the steep tax on the rich is causing the big problem of high unemployment, cutting those taxes will allow the rich to create more jobs, providing more families with the ability to put food on their tables. Failure to act will maintain the high rate of unemployment, keeping people impoverished.

STAGE THREE
Harness active support

P resent the solution from the clandestine agenda as effective, socially justified, and as a unique approach that solves a big, important problem. In the end, call for action.

The Main Points

The secret weapon strategies:

The secret weapon strategy: Phase one
Provide a big incentive to decision makers that is most relevant for achieving your goal.

The secret weapon strategy: Phase two
Exploit a big, real problem that exists in society and connect it to the agenda. The problem will be fully tailored to correspond with the provided solution.

The secret weapon strategy: Phase three
Explain in a logical way (cause and effect) why the solution is effective in solving the problem.

The secret weapon strategy: Phase four
Legitimize the private agenda (sometimes a clandestine one.) Present the given solution as

socially justified: as a solution that makes the world a better place.

The secret weapon strategy: Phase five

Build a call to action that is based on a dichotomy. Present a solution with only two options, where one option is good and the other is bad.

Chapter 6

The Game Changers
Five powerful tools of rhetoric

The effective delivery of a public agenda should contain five elements for harnessing active support. The first element is that the solution presented in the agenda creates a big impact by solving a large, important problem. The second element is a logical explanation that explains why implementing the solution will be effective in solving the problem. The third element is that the solution is justified socially and will make the world a better place. The fourth element is that the specific solution on offer is unique. The fifth element is a call to action that presents the solution as a choice between two options, where one option is good and the other is bad.

The five powerful tools of rhetoric

Big impact

The solution must grab our attention and answer the question of why we should invest our limited resources of time, money, and mental energy in the proposed agenda. The big impact is processed by our primitive lizard mind. It evokes our emotions, and the message stays in our memory for a long time. To effectively deliver the solution – and its proposed benefits – in a presentation, we have to paint a vivid picture of the big impact.

For example, it is one thing to say that there is a climate crisis. But it's more impactful to zoom in and paint a picture of a polar bear in the North Pole that can swim over 100 miles from one glacier to another in the cold ocean. In today's climate, however, the polar bear will likely drown, as the warming temperatures and melting glaciers have extended the distance between glaciers to over 150 miles. This painting of a vivid picture impacts us emotionally. And because it evokes our emotions, the message remains imprinted in our memory.

Effectiveness

We have to create a logical explanation, a theory of cause and effect, that will convince people of the solution's effectiveness, as processed by our logical/analytical mind. We must showcase why our promoted solution is feasible, practical, and effective in solving the problem.

For example, if a new digital bank wants to acquire new customers, the bank can offer big incentives for new customers to open a bank account. The new digital bank can offer high interest rates on deposits and an exemption from commissions. Here, the logic is that people respond to incentives and this is why using this method will be effective in producing positive results.

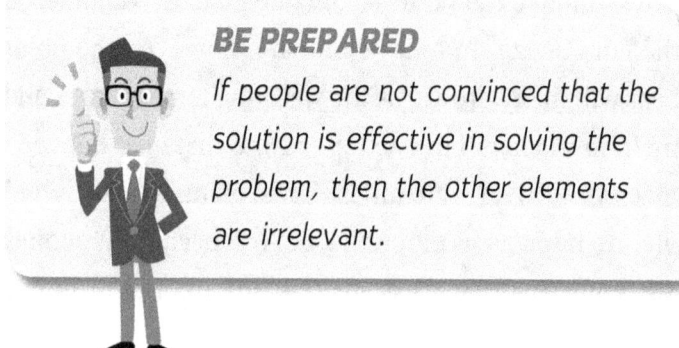

BE PREPARED

If people are not convinced that the solution is effective in solving the problem, then the other elements are irrelevant.

Justified socially

Solutions – even effective ones that solve a big problem – can often produce other problems. Therefore, even if a solution creates a social problem, we have to justify its use. We must show that the added value of implementing the solution is greater than any possible problems.

For example, putting cameras on cops as a solution to considerably reduce their violence against citizens. By equipping on-duty cops with cameras, we compromise their right to personal privacy. But if we weigh the enormous benefits of using the cameras – that is, reduced violence – then we can justify the solution.

BE AWARE!
The public justification is based on the prevailing norms of a given society.

Uniqueness

Processed by our wisdom, judgment offers direction – like a compass – to choose one specific solution over another. When we want to show the uniqueness of our solution, we have to highlight the traits that exist in our solution that do not exist elsewhere.

For example, the textile industry consumes a lot of clean water to produce its products, including jeans. There are many companies that offer a good solution to this by solving the water usage problem. However, the fabric that is produced when using this solution is of low quality. Fortunately, there is another company with a solution that addresses the water usage problem while producing high-quality fabric. Therefore, their solution is unique and exclusive only to their product.

BE PREPARED

In reality, our challenge in the decision-making process is to compare given solutions and then choose the best option for our specific needs.

Dichotomy

Processed by our lizard mind, if we are presented with only two options, our ability to make a quick decision is much greater than when we have more than two alternatives. Therefore, if we want to build an effective call to action, the solution Should be presented as a dichotomy. Present a solution with only two options, where one option is right and the other is wrong.

"You take the blue pill — the story ends, you wake up in your bed and believe whatever you want to believe. You take the red pill — you stay in Wonderland, and I show you how deep the rabbit hole goes."

— *Morpheus, The Matrix*

The Main Points

Big impact

The solution must grab our attention and address, why we should invest in it our limited resources of time, money, and mental energy.

Effectiveness

We must create a logical explanation, a theory of cause and effect, that will convince people why the solution is effective.

Justified socially

Even if a solution creates a social problem, we have to explain why using it is justified.

Uniqueness

When we want to show the uniqueness of our solution, we have to highlight the traits that exist in our solution that do not exist elsewhere.

74

Dichotomy

If we want to build an effective call to action, the solution should be presented as a dichotomy. Present a solution with only two options, where one option is right and the other is wrong.

Chapter 7

Play It Safe
How to avoid manipulation

Unlike the perfect world, where people's public and personal agendas are the same, in the real world, people and entities have a personal clandestine agenda that differs from their public one. In the real world, these people and entities see others as objects – simply as tools whose sole purpose is to serve *their* personal desires and goals, even at the expense of the wants and needs of others.

While their public agenda seemingly represents the prevailing desires and values of those in society, their private agenda may, in fact, be wildly different. If we are not able to identify the various types of manipulation used by these people and entities, we impair our ability to make effective decisions. More than that, we will invest our limited resources of time, money, and mental energy on things that don't serve our values and desires.

We have two lines of defense to enable us to invest our limited resources on agendas that serve *our* personal desires and values.

The first line of defense: Before we adopt the agenda
Use critical thinking

There are five powerful tools of rhetoric they will use to try to gain our active support. We must question and cast doubt on each one of these powerful tools of rhetoric.

First tool of rhetoric: Big Impact

The first tool of rhetoric that people and entities will use to gain active support for their agenda is this: they will say that if we actively support their agenda, it will have a big, positive impact on our lives – that it will solve an important problem we currently face.

How to cast doubt

Do not automatically believe the big-impact claim. We have to consider the options that are present in the status quo before we adopt the solution. Evaluate whether there are existing solutions that can offer a good resolution to the problem without using the solution purported in their agenda.

For example, a blood test shows that we don't have enough vitamin D in our blood. We can buy pills that contain vitamin D, but we can also expose ourselves to the sun for 15 minutes a day. Therefore, the vitamin D pills can have an impact on our health, but the impact isn't very big because we can also use an alternative, natural solution.

Second tool of rhetoric: Effectiveness

The second tool of rhetoric that they use for harnessing active support is to give a logical explanation for the effectiveness of the solution, and to illustrate how it will solve the problem we are facing.

How to cast doubt

See if the explanation/theory is supported by empirical evidence.

For example, we are seeking a contractor to build our house. We interview five contractors for the project. One of them impressed us more than the others. Is that enough? No. Perhaps he only impressed us because he has strong presentation skills. Therefore, we must reach out to some of his former clients and inquire about his qualifications, skills, and level of trustworthiness.

Third tool of rhetoric: Socially Justified

The third tool of rhetoric they use is to show that their solution is socially justified and will make the world a better place.

How to cast doubt

Often, even when a solution is effective, it, itself, can create a problem.

For example, the government can create endless business regulations. At first glance, this may sound good because it supposedly protects the consumer. However, additional regulations can cost the business owner a lot of money. Therefore, the business owner has two options: close their business or roll over the extra costs to the consumer.

Fourth tool of rhetoric: Uniqueness

The fourth tool of rhetoric is to convey that their solution is unique and has qualities that other solutions do not.

How to cast doubt

To reveal the falsehoods behind the entities' claims of uniqueness, we must evaluate the proposed solution against the available alternatives and decide which we prefer.

For example, a food company charged more money for its product because they added vitamin C to it. They charged 20 percent more than their competitors. But, there are other companies that add vitamin C to their products without the 20 percent price increase. Therefore, the proposed product is not unique and there is no justification for the additional 20 percent.

Fifth tool of rhetoric: Dichotomous Choice

Their fifth tool of rhetoric for convincing us to support their agenda is to have us believe that we are faced with only two options: the "right one," to invest our limited resources in their agenda and win; or the "wrong one," to reject their agenda and lose.

How to cast doubt

Check if we are facing a false dichotomy. For example, if a doctor gives us medical advice that presents a choice of only two options, then we must get a second opinion – or even a third one, if necessary.

Can we trust the entities that promote their agenda?

Let's suppose the entities (corporations or people) succeed in convincing us with these five powerful tools of rhetoric that we will benefit tremendously from actively supporting their agenda. At this stage, the big question we have to ask ourselves is this: Can this persuasive person or entity be trusted? If the person or entity does not have a strong moral basis, then it will not be a good idea to support their agenda. All the rhetoric and empirical evidence that they use to convince us to support their agenda will likely not produce the result we expect and desire.

The second line of defense: After we adopt the agenda

After you have decided to take action and adopt the agenda, your second line of defense is to protect yourself by adopting five risk management practices.

"Risk comes from not knowing what you are doing."

— *Warren Buffett*

We have five powerful tools that will protect us in a manipulative world of immoral people or entities.

Here are the tools:

- First, acquire **knowledge**.
- Second, if needed, get advice from **trusted** external experts.
- Third, practice **diversification**. Don't invest all your resources in one agenda.
- Fourth, maintain **control** of your investment.
- Fifth, **supervise** their activities.

BE PREPARED

These five powerful tools will protect us from those who seek to manipulate us.

If, for example, we are talking about the financial world, first gain knowledge to understand what exactly you are doing with your money. Second, if somebody tries to persuade you to transfer your money to a bank account that is not in your name, don't do it, because you will lose control and supervision of your money. And if somebody tries to convince you to invest in binary options, don't do that either because it doesn't have any supervision.

The Main Points

We understand that when we are in the realm of human behavior, we cannot *a priori* know what will happen. Therefore, we have to approach any person or entity that tries to harness our limited resources of time, money, and mental energy with full awareness, using the two lines of defense.

The first line of defense: Before we adopt the agenda

Adopt critical thinking before you act. There are five powerful tools of rhetoric for getting our active support. We have to question and cast doubt on each of them. We also have to ask ourselves if the entities promoting the agenda can be trusted.

The second line of defense: After we adopt the agenda

Protect yourself with the five risk management practices: knowledge, trustworthiness, diversification, control, and supervision.

Chapter 8

Generate Long-Term Income
Invest your money wisely

Having a good income is not always enough to secure your economic future: for that, you also have to build an investment portfolio that will generate long-term income.

The process of building wealth is simple:

Make money

Save money

Invest money

In principle, there are three major channels for investing your money:

Option one: Bank products

Deposits, savings plans, or structures.

This is a good option for when your general investment knowledge is low or when the interest rates are high and you have a lot of uncertainty and volatility in both the financial and real estate markets.

Option two: Invest in financial instruments

Invest in securities: bonds, stocks, and commodities. To do this, you must acquire knowledge.

Option three: Real investment

Money invested in tangible and productive assets such as plant machinery and real estate, as opposed to investment in securities or other financial instruments.

To do this, you must acquire deep knowledge.

What is your biggest expense each year?

If you have money that you can save but you don't have the knowledge to invest it wisely, you lose money. Why? Because if you had the knowledge, you could earn a lot more.

The following examples will reveal two common occurrences in the world of investments.

The investment advisors

L et's consider two financial advisors who work in the same bank, in the same branch and department. They both have professional, high-level qualifications, but one represents behavior as seen in the perfect-world, while the other reflects real-world behavior.

Investment Advisor A: Represents perfect-world behavior

H is moral compass is calibrated toward behaving honestly; he sees his customers as goals in themselves and not only as a means to achieve his private desires and goals. Therefore, his main purpose is to serve his clients' desires and goals, even if it means he will be considered an inferior advisor to Advisor B.

Investment Advisor B: Represents real-world behavior

A dvisor B's top priority is fulfilling his desires and goals, even at the expense of his clients' desires and goals.

Scenario one: Win-win

Let's assume a customer comes to the advisors' department with an investment portfolio that needs an overhaul. In this case, Advisor A will act accordingly and make the necessary changes. In the process, they will buy and sell securities as needed.

The bank they work in will enjoy the large commissions that result from these investment activities. The client also enjoys the professional advice that he received to improve his investment portfolio.

The advisor's desires were to get commissions for the bank and provide the client with professional advice. The customer's need was to get professional advice. Both parties served as means to an end but they also helped the other achieve their goals. This is a win-win situation.

Scenario two: Win-lose

Now let's assume a different scenario. A client has an investment portfolio that doesn't need any changes at all. If this client came to Advisor A, he would say, "Your portfolio doesn't require any changes. See you next time."

Let's assume that instead, he came to Advisor B who, professionally, thinks like Advisor A: that no change is needed.

However, Advisor B would offer this client the bad and immoral advice to buy and sell securities. His purpose is to bring commissions to his department at the client's expense.

If Advisor B repeats this unethical behavior day after day, then he will likely generate higher commissions for his department than Advisor A.

And if Advisor B's manager holds the same moral values, then the likelihood of Advisor B receiving bonuses and a promotion are much greater than for Advisor A.

Advisor A could practice the same immoral behavior as Advisor B. But he is willing to pay the price for practicing the value of honesty, even if it harms his economic status in the bank where he works, and also hurts his family economically.

Advisor B, because of his immoral behavior, gets a larger salary and more bonuses, and there is a higher likelihood that he will be promoted to department manager.

If the real agenda of the bank policy was that their

clients are more important than the commissions, then in such an imaginary world, Advisor A would be the winner.

BE PREPARED

Of course, if the client was aware of the situation with Advisor B, he would never agree to operate according to his advice.

The public agenda:
"Your desires are my goal"

Both the morally good advisor (A) and the morally bad advisor (B) will always introduce themselves as advisors who put their clients' goals and desires first.

The reason is obvious. This is what we all want to hear and believe – it's music to our ears.

BE AWARE!
It is important to note that what makes Advisor B's advice bad and immoral isn't the practical results but his original intention.

Morality always refers to the intention, not the end result. There could be a situation where Advisor B's unethical advice will, in retrospect, give good results on the investments of the client, but our focus should be on his original intention to use the customer as a means to achieve his selfish desires.

Another key note is that, in reality, people do not act in dichotomous ways – they can behave in ways that fall between these two worlds. Perhaps if Advisor B has a client who understands the world of investments, he will behave differently.

In conclusion, it is essential that you acquire knowledge of investments. This will protect your money from immoral people and enable you to meet your financial goals.

The real investment offer

A private company with major investments in real estate offers well-established investors to join their real estate projects in the US. The company's presenter explains their business model to the prospective investors.

Each year the company is involved in over 100 real estate projects in the US. The prospective investor can choose in which specific project to invest their money, and it should be a minimum investment of half a million dollars.

After five years, the company takes 30 percent of the profit for projects that succeed. An investor in the audience asks, "What happens to my money if the project fails?" The presenter says to him, "I will answer you privately after the presentation."

The main model presented here is this: you, as an investor, assume the risk of losing all your invested money if the project fails. While the private company will not bear the loss, they will share the profits with you if your project succeeds. This kind of business model is very common in the world of real investments.

BE PREPARED

Before you invest in real investments — such as a startup company or a real estate project — ensure your level of knowledge and trust are high.

Investor rules to adopt to build and preserve your wealth

Rule one: Acquire knowledge

Without the right investment knowledge, you stand a high chance of being manipulated.

The knowledge you acquire enables you to build a private investment portfolio that will generate long-term income.

Rule two: Don't make hasty decisions

An investor who displays patience and restraint will be more successful than an investor who lacks these qualities.

Rule three: Diversify

The safest way to invest your money is to apply the famous golden rule: "Don't put all your eggs in one basket." If you practice diversification, even a stock market crash shouldn't worry you too much.

Invest Your Money
1/3 in Stocks & Bonds
1/3 in Real Estate & Commodities
1/3 in Liquid Assets

"Success in investing doesn't correlate with IQ... what you need is the temperament to control the urges that get other people into trouble in investing."

— *Warren Buffett*

The Main Points

Having a good income is not always enough to secure your economic future: for that, you also have to build an investment portfolio that will generate long-term income.

In the financial markets, you must acquire investment knowledge. This will protect your money from immoral people and enable you to achieve your financial goals.

Before you invest in real investments — such as a startup company or a real estate company — ensure your level of knowledge and trust are high.

Chapter 9

Become Enlightened
Use the secret weapon

Even when living in a liberal democratic country that acts according to the social contract and gives us the freedom to do what we want (if acting from our free will and not harming others), this liberty alone is not enough.

Make *your* world a better place

To achieve our goals and live the life we truly want, we need money. A dream life can mean different things to different people. It could be owning a house near the beach in a safe, quiet neighborhood; traveling the globe to experience new people and cultures; sending our children to good schools; or having the financial ability to help others. These goals – and many more – are often limited by the amount of money we earn and possess.

Make the world a better place

The secret weapon also enables us to promote agendas that connect to our values and beliefs. Even if promoting social agendas does not directly enhance our financial status, the ability to support social causes that we care about bolsters our overall sense of well-being. Human beings are holistic, and to enhance our mental strength and energy, we must act in ways that align with our core values and beliefs – in ways that support other people in our society.

Financial independence

The holy grail of *Perfect World, Real World* is to give you the best tools for becoming financially independent. To achieve the goal of financial independence, you must possess three important abilities. While these abilities were presented in detail in previous chapters, here we offer a concluding snapshot of the three key abilities.

Three must-have abilities to achieve financial independence

Ability one:
Identify manipulations and say no

The first ability you must possess in order to become financially independent is to identify manipulations and to say no to them. When we say no to entities (people or corporations) that seek to manipulate us and exploit our limited resources of time, money, and mental energy, we can instead use those limited resources to say yes to other agendas – those that serve our values, goals, and desires.

Ability two:
Harness active support for your agenda

The second ability you must possess in order to become financially independent is to harness active support for your agenda. The five strategies of the secret weapon enable you to promote agendas that serve your goals. These strategies can be used to gain a higher position in your workplace; raise money for your startup company; effectively promote your business's product or service; or to endorse a social agenda that connects to your core values and beliefs.

Ability three:
Build and preserve your wealth

The third ability you must possess in order to become financially independent is to build and preserve your wealth. The ability to earn money from working alone is not enough. Having the right tools and knowledge to manage a private investment portfolio that includes stocks, bonds, real estate, and commodities creates significant passive income.

BE AWARE!

Most well-established people gained their wealth from their investments, not their income.

Enlightenment

Being enlightened is to be freed from ignorance and misinformation. It is to show understanding, act in a positive, reasonable manner, and to not follow false or outdated beliefs.

To be an enlightened person

In the 17th century, the great philosopher Immanuel Kant wrote an article on what it means to be enlightened. One of his most striking observations was that if you take two people with the same cognitive abilities, but where one is enlightened and the other is not, *the only reason* that the enlightened person experiences greater benefits is because they decided to use their reasoning. The same goes for the secret weapon strategies: if you take two people with the same abilities and one uses the secret weapon strategies and the other does not, the difference between them can be enormous.

The Main Points

The secret weapon strategies give you the tools and knowledge you need to gain enlightenment on how to achieve financial independence. Compared to those who don't take advantage of them, using the strategies of the secret weapon will help you achieve your goals so you can live financially independent and free.

Part Two:

Promoting
Social Issues

Chapter 10

Promote Social Agendas

Make the world a better place

Until now, the strategies of the secret weapon were mainly used to enhance your ability to promote economic matters. Success in doing so helps bring about financial independence. But the strategies of the secret weapon can also be used to effectively promote social agendas that are important to you. And while promoting these social agendas is not likely to make you wealthier, it can definitely make you feel happier and more complete.

A moral problem

A moral problem arises in any situation that involves a conflict of interest between two or more people. If there isn't a conflict of interest, there isn't a moral problem. If at least one person in the conflict sees another as only a means to an end and uses means of enforcement, deceit, or threat to get what they want, then the conflict becomes a moral problem.

The classroom supervisor

Suppose you are a supervisor in a class of students who are taking a history exam. Your mission is to supervise the students so that they do not cheat. During the exam, you see that one of the students in the class looks at notes he has prepared in advance. Your first thought is to ignore what you saw. In the worst-case scenario, this student will get a higher grade. You figure that this is not a big deal, and therefore that it shouldn't concern you. Another option, however, is to confront him. You think to yourself that perhaps doing so isn't worth it. This line of thought can lead to passive behavior, acting as if everything is ok in the class you supervised.

But when we consider this scenario on a deeper moral level, we realize something else: there are other students in the class who aren't using prepared notes, granting the cheating student an unfair advantage. Because of this, perhaps in the near future when these students apply to prestigious universities, the implication of your passive behavior is that the cheating student may be accepted at the expense of a non-cheating student because of his higher grades. Now, upon reflection, you realize the moral conflict and its implications.

The true meaning of passive action is acting in an immoral way: not doing anything has bad implications. Now, as the classroom supervisor, you profoundly understand that by ignoring the situation and not stopping the student who cheats, there is a high chance that you will take an active role in hurting the students who were honest and obedient. It is likely that because of your new understanding and awareness of the moral implications of your behavior, you will have a moral incentive to act differently: you will confront the cheating student.

Get classroom supervisors to fulfill their role

With the above example in mind, if I am now in a position to hire supervisors, before I send them to supervise classes, I give them a short lecture on the moral implications of not doing their job properly. This will increase the probability that they will fulfill their role, as they will be morally incentivized to do their job properly.

> **BE AWARE!**
> One of the secret weapon strategies is using incentives to actively promote our agenda; we presume that people can be incentivized to change their behavior.

From the example, we see that moral implications can be used as a powerful incentive that impacts our behavior. We also learn from that example that moral conflict and its implications are not always clear at first glance. Therefore, we are obligated – if we want to promote our agenda – to make things clear and not expect that people will automatically do the right thing.

The agenda:

Arm teachers in schools with guns

The big problem

There is gun violence in schools. In most incidents, many students and teachers are killed or wounded.

Why people are being killed

When the attacker comes to a school with a gun, in most cases, they are not confronted by anyone within the first few minutes. Most of the time, even if there are guards at school, they will prefer to protect their own life and not confront the attacker directly. On average, it takes six to ten minutes for the police to arrive on the scene. Therefore, the attacker encounters a "soft target," and until the police arrive, the attacker can kill and injure many people without anyone standing in their way.

Because most of the deaths and injuries occur in the first few minutes, there are two critical elements to reduce the number of fatalities and injuries: improve response time and give weapons to the people who are willing to directly confront the attacker.

The solution

We must equip trained teachers in schools with guns. Teachers with guns have the ability to respond immediately when there is a gun attack in the school. Of equal importance is that, if necessary, they will put their lives at risk and confront the attacker, saving the lives of their beloved students.

What makes this solution unique?

This is the only solution on the table that will give us a real-time response. This is essential in a life-or-death situation where every second counts. When paired with the willingness of the armed teachers to confront the attacker directly and risk their own lives, this solution will drastically reduce the number of injuries and fatalities.

The teachers' union can justifiably resist the agenda that teachers in school should carry guns to protect their students. They will claim that a teacher should be a teacher and nothing else.

Therefore, the unique justification as presented above can be the game changer that will persuade the union to change their mind.

Violent Cops

The problem

Cops' violent behavior decreases citizens' trust in, and cooperation with, the police force. It hurts their main mission: to catch and jail criminals and make the streets safer by preventing future crimes.

The solution

The cops will be equipped with bodycams that are active while they are on duty. The cameras will be a compelling incentive for the cops to not act violently. If they display violence, their behavior will be recorded and used to incriminate them.

BE PREPARED

To promote the agenda, we must demonstrate why the solution is morally justified.

The solution produces a moral problem: a clash between the value of the cops' privacy versus the public's right to safety and security.

We can claim that the price the cops pay is not so terrible because they are required to wear the camera only while on duty. The added value to the public's safety wildly outweighs the cops' discomfort of having to where a bodycam. Therefore, equipping on-duty cops with cameras is justified.

The farmer and the intruder

The problem

A farmer sees a thief trying to intrude on his land and steal his farm machines.

The solution

From the standpoint of the farmer
Killing the intruder will be appropriate and morally justified. It would also deter other intruders from trespassing.

Farmer's justification for killing the intruder

For the farmer, the value of owning property is greater than the value of life.

In a liberal democratic society, there isn't a justification to kill the intruder if they can instead be neutralized.

The norm in a democratic society

While norms can differ depending on the society, in a liberal democratic society you may: shoot the intruder if they try to kill you and your life is in danger, or if you must protect yourself or others. But if you shoot them and now they are neutralized, you don't have the legal or moral right to keep shooting until they die.

The value here is that the life of a human being (even if they tried to steal your property) is more important than owning property.

In a liberal democratic society, the only justification that gives you the right to take the life of another person is if your life or the innocent life of others are in danger.

In another society

In another country, the norms could be different: if someone intrudes on your land and tries to steal your property, you have the moral right to kill them. In this country, the norm dictates that the value of owning property is greater than the value of life itself.

BE PREAPERED

When we promote an agenda, the justification should be based on the prevailing norms of the given society.

The Main Points

The strategies of the secret weapon can also be used to effectively promote social agendas that are important to you. While promoting social agendas is not likely to make you wealthier, it can definitely make you feel happier and more complete.

Chapter 11

What You See is What You Get

Empirical evidence

> "Everything works in PowerPoint; but if you have the physical item or some demonstration software, that's much more convincing to people than a PowerPoint presentation or a business plan."

> — *Elon Musk*

A s we saw in previous chapters, if someone uses (or we use) powerful rhetorical tools effectively, they can convince others to make nearly any choice. Therefore, the next step is to question if the argument is objectively sound – or if the person making the presentation is simply a compelling presenter. The first line of defense is to check the credibility of their argument by seeing if there is empirical evidence to support their assertions.

The vegetarian's lioness

Premise A: All lions are vegetarians.
Premise B: The dog that I own is a lion.
Conclusion: My dog is a vegetarian.

From the example we can see that all the arguments are false. But if somebody adopts the two (false) arguments as true and doesn't question their credibility by using empirical observation, then they must also accept the (false) conclusion as true. This is called the validity of an argument.

BE AWARE!
In rational scientific thinking, empirical evidence is used to test if assumptions are true or false — that is, it's used to test an argument's validity.

Pre-modern science

In modern society, using empirical evidence as a tool is common practice. However, in ancient times and the Middle Ages, most worldly insights were drawn only from rational logical thinking, not rational empirical thinking. This approach, called rationalism, purported that you can learn about the nature of the world without conducting observations but instead by using only pure logic.

Therefore, before modern science, arguments about the world were based purely on logical thinking – without any empirical evidence to support their claims.

Aristotle and the falling objects

Aristotle claimed that when different objects fall to earth, their speed will be fixed and dependent on their mass. Therefore, if an object has a greater mass, it will reach the ground faster.

Aristotle didn't empirically check the trueness of his claim. For him, if it sounded reasonable, then it must be objectively true.

Amazingly, for nearly 2,000 years, Aristotle's

false claim was considered true and remained unchallenged.

Until, in the early 17th century, Galileo Galilei found that objects fall at a changing speed and that their speed is not dependent on their mass. So, a heavy and a light object will reach the earth at the same time.

Those findings contradicted Aristotle's claim. But more importantly, they also introduced a powerful tool to the world: empirical evidence.

Galileo conducted empirical observations. He threw different objects with different masses from a tower and measured their speed. He found that they reached the ground at the same time. The meaning of this empirical finding was that their speeds were the same even if their masses were different.

Science's giant steps

From the 17th century onward, empiricism replaced rational logical thinking as the main tool used in modern science for learning about the world.

Instead of intelligence-based rational thinking, great thinkers began using their senses to gain worldly knowledge and insights.

Science developed very slowly until the 17th century. But from the moment that we began favoring empiricism (senses-based observations) over arguments based on speculation and intuition, science developed in leaps and bounds.

The businessperson and the professors

A businessperson introduced a challenge to marketing professors at a prestigious business school: "Please build me a model of how to choose the best channels for advertising my products. I spend a lot of advertising dollars, but I prefer to invest my money in the most profitable, effective channels."

The next day, before the professors found an effective solution for the challenge, the businessperson called them and said, "I no longer need your services; I have solved the problem myself.

"My solution is very simple: I asked the clients who arrived at my business where they first heard about my product. Therefore, based on this empirical evidence collected from my customers, I now know the most effective channels for publishing my services. Based on the empirical results, I identified where to effectively invest my advertising dollars."

The olive oil factory

Imagine you are on a trip and along the way you stop at an olive oil factory. The owner gives a lecture about the quality of their oil. They enthusiastically explain that their family has been in the olive oil industry for 150 years. They give you a tour of their olive grove and present reliable certifications showing their first-place wins in various international competitions.

Their aim is to persuade you to buy their oil. Their explanations and the empirical evidence that supports their claims are used to convince you that they have the capability and know-how to produce oil to the industry's highest standards.

Now you have to decide if you want to buy their oil. You ask yourself: What will determine if the oil that I purchase is really of high quality?

The answer: only the owner's morality. Even if they can produce high-quality oil, they know that to gain a big profit from you and other clients, they must mix their high-quality oil with cheap oil. By doing so, their profits will increase threefold. With over 200 clients per day, there is a lot of money involved here.

The owner knows that this kind of immoral behavior will bring them a lot of happiness because it will support their goals and desires. By practicing this immoral behavior, the owner can financially support their daughter, who wants to attend a prestigious university abroad, and indulge in life's luxuries by buying themselves a fancy sports car.

On the other hand, we can think of another person with the same professionalism and experience who chooses to stick to moral behavior – the virtue of integrity – and sells pure oil that isn't cut with cheap olive oil. Their profitability will be considerably less compared to the first person. This person chooses to act on the basis of honesty, and leads a life according to the values of fairness and integrity.

We, as buyers, have a legitimate desire to buy 100 percent high-quality oil. To achieve this goal, we can use our intuition to decide if we trust the seller or not. But there is something else we can do: if we have the knowledge, we can test the oil to empirically know its quality and therefore make the right decision that serves our goals and desires.

Customer recommendations

These days, there are companies that serve as mediators between freelancers who provide services and customers who want to use their services. One of the most important tools is getting feedback from their customers on the freelancers' quality of service. These recommendations provide empirical evidence on the quality of the service provided. If, for example, I see a plumber with over 1,000 positive recommendations, I assume that even if I haven't used his service in the past, I can trust him. The recommendations compel me to believe that he is professional and reliable.

The Main Points

When we encounter an entity that uses powerful rhetorical tools to harness active support for a certain agenda, one of the first lines of defense against possible manipulation is to check the entity's credibility. This means seeing if there is empirical evidence to support the entity's claims. Finding such empirical evidence will enable us to make decisions that serve our interests and goals.

Chapter 12

Personal Values
Discerning good from bad

In the previous chapter, we discussed the importance of empirical evidence, which can prove the validity of an argument. But for harnessing active support, sometimes empirical evidence is not enough. We also have to demonstrate its morality. To show the effectiveness of something, we must use rational thinking, but deciding if something is good or bad depends on our values and beliefs.

Let's explore these concepts using examples.

The gun factory

If we consider a gun factory and discuss the procedure to produce quality effective guns, we are using rational thinking. If we can show after the gun was manufactured that it is of high quality, this still does not answer the value question of whether it is good or bad to produce more guns.

Some people will say that producing more guns is great because they offer protection. Others say that producing more guns is bad because their mere existence begets violence.

People can observe the same data and think and act differently because their values and beliefs can be different.

BE AWARE!

It is our values and belief systems that color our understanding of whether something is good or bad.

A permanent lunar military base

The United States Space Force (USSF) is the sixth branch of the United States Armed Forces. Its main goal is to control military operations in outer space.

Let's suppose that one of the USSF's first missions is to build a permanent military base on the moon.

This will give the United States a tremendous military advantage over all other countries. To

133

check the feasibility of this project, they summon international experts in a variety of fields. After the experts check the data, they agree unanimously that the project is possible. However, executing the project will require huge amounts of money.

Therefore, the question is now: Where will the money come from? The health budget, the education budget, the welfare budget, higher taxes?

While it is clearly possible (to build a permanent lunar military base), now the crucial question is this: Do we want to? The answer to this question doesn't have a unanimous opinion.

There are people who will claim that the value of education and health care are much higher than the value of building a military base on the moon.

There will be others, such as those in government, who will claim that not building a military base will compromise the future of American life.

When we asked the first question about whether it is possible, the answer was dependent on what we or the experts know. The second question, however, is not dependent on what we know. Instead, it depends entirely on what we want – it depends on our values and desires.

BE PREPARED

When we have a dilemma about which goal, we should pursue, scientific rational thinking will not help us decide.

Scientific rational thinking will help us only when we know in advance the goal we want to pursue. Then the rational scientific thinking will help us by giving us the best means to do it in an effective and efficient way.

The flooded cave

Suppose that you are in an underground cave and your guide receives an emergency message from a meteorologic station that in one hour the cave will be flooded due to heavy rains. Everyone in the cave knows that if they want to survive, they have to exit the cave as soon as possible. But there can be a situation where all of the people in the cave except one will want to escape.

There is a person in the cave who knows what we

135

all know, but prefers to stay because for him the value of life is worthless.

In the world of science, we know that water must boil in 100°C and things in the gravitational field must fall. But in the world of values and value-derived decisions, everything we do comes from our choice; nothing is a must.

Even people's decision to escape the cave isn't trivial. It is based on a value. They choose to do it because they want to live. Their behavior dictates that life has value. But someone who doesn't believe in the value of life can choose to stay in the cave and die. For them, life doesn't have value. We can see from the behavior of the man in the cave that even our physical existence isn't always a clear target; our physical existence depends on the value that we attach to life. We can see two people who know the same facts (like the people in the cave) but who make different decisions based on their values and beliefs.

From the above examples, we can see scientific rational thinking as the ability to analyze data and situations. But it is our values and desires that ultimately guide our practical decisions, behavior, and course of action.

In the rational world, we ask if the process of manufacturing a gun is an effective and efficient one. But for deciding if guns should be produced in the first place, we must question the morality of the decision based on our values and desires. The answer to whether a process is effective depends on objective data. It does not depend on the personality of the one making the argument. But the moral question of gun production depends solely on the person's values and desires.

Scientific rational thinking is objective and not dependent on people's character. We use scientific thinking to choose the most efficient and effective way to carry out our goals. Values and desires give us the ability to choose which goals we want to pursue, and shape whether those goals are considered by us and the society in which we live as morally good or bad.

Values vs. scientific thinking

Values and desires determine the goals we want to pursue. They answer the question of which path we choose to walk in life. Decisions are based on our subjective values and beliefs. We can decide to act

137

in a moral way; we can take into account norms based on the moral codes of the society in which we live and behave according to them. We can also choose to behave immorally.

Scientific thinking can be used as a tool to clarify the most effective way to carry out a goal. To decide how to move from point A to point B and achieve our values and desires, we will use rational thinking to find the most efficient and effective way. We can build and use a method based on cause and effect and validate it with empirical data. This method is objective and relevant to all people, no matter their values and beliefs.

Moral values, expressed in our behavior toward others, are the compass for deciding how we pursue our goals. Morality gives the guidelines for how to achieve our goals within the confines of the norms and laws of the society in which we live.

The Main Points

Values and desires define the path we choose to walk — the goals we want to pursue.

Rational empirical thinking creates an effective method for achieving a given goal.

Moral values, expressed in our behavior toward others, are our compass for deciding how we pursue our goals.

Chapter 13

Freedom of Choice

Succeeding in the challenging social environment

> "Decision makers can satisfice either by finding optimum solutions for a simplified world, or by finding satisfactory solutions for a more realistic world."
>
> — *Herbert Simon*

The conceptual basis for the existence of the democratic state is the "social contract." The claim of Jean-Jacques Rousseau, who introduced the idea of the social contract, is that the natural state of human beings is to do what we want – that is, to be autonomous.

The social contract

At some point in our development, we realized that it would be easier for us to survive if we all entered into a "contract" in which we would give up some of our freedoms for the benefit of the collective, and in order to receive other benefits in return. For example, we give up the freedoms to say, take, and do whatever we want in favor of the possibility of living in security. To ensure that the social contract will be fulfilled in practice, we created an artificial entity, which we called a "state," and appointed a part of the population to manage it. We gave power and authority to this managing entity, which we called "government," to act in our favor and protect the interests of all. Remember that *we* are sovereign and the government should work for us, not the other way around. They are obligated to exercise the powers we have given them only for our benefit.

The government must not violate our freedoms without just cause. If, for example, I commented on someone's haircut and they were offended, this is not a damaging enough act to justify an infringement on my right to practice freedom of speech. Democracy is based on this principle. If the government violates this principle and interferes in our lives without just cause, then we would not, in fact, live in a democratic state but a dictatorship.

An example to illustrate freedom of choice

The argument: Not allowing marijuana use violates the democratic freedom of choice principle.

Freedom of choice is a key democratic principle. The democratic system is based on the logic that all human beings know how to choose what is best for themselves. One of the social contract's central principles is that the government has the right to limit a person's choice in only two cases: when that person harms another, or when they make an irrational decision (from a state of cognitive impairment) that causes self-harm or that was made under coercion.

Smoking marijuana does not meet those principles. If I smoke in my private house and don't drive after that, then I'm not hurting anyone. Second, as an adult, I have the right to prioritize damages. Even if smoking marijuana shortens my life expectancy, I have the right to decide that the pleasure it causes me is worth it. Moreover, it is very similar to the situation where I choose to eat unhealthy food, drink alcohol, or engage in extreme sports. It is my right to decide that I prefer to enjoy life now – even at the detriment of my life expectancy. Therefore, forbidding me to smoke marijuana is an unjustified violation of my freedom of choice according to the principles of managing a society in a democratic country.

What is the big impact?

Freedom of choice in a democratic country is one of the main principles that allows us, as citizens, to lead our lives as we wish. Let's say that our choice was made rationally, without coercion or harm to self or others. But if, in this instance, I let the government forbid me to do as I wish, then, by extension, I'm permitting the government to do this in other areas as well. The government can use the same logic to tell me what to eat, drink, read, wear, etc. The freedom of choice principle is my main shield against such infringements.

Expressing an opposing position

We can challenge the basic premise of the argument that smoking marijuana does not harm anyone other than the smoker. We can argue that marijuana, in most cases, is a gateway drug that can quickly lead a person to using – and become addicted to – more dangerous drugs, such as heroin and cocaine. Moreover, the drug effects will impair the judgment of the addict, increasing the chances that they will harm those around him, including friends and family members. Therefore, as members of a society, we prefer to let the government infringe on our freedom of choice in the case of marijuana, but we have justification to do so.

The decision-making process

The lizard brain is the most primitive part of the brain. By extension, any part of a person's psyche or personality can be dominated by instinct or impulse rather than rational thought. When we encounter a problem that can have a big impact on our lives, this part of our brain will trigger our emotions and motivate us to act.

Wisdom (our compass) is connected to our core values, morality, and beliefs. It is responsible for deciding the direction we want to move in – the goals we want to pursue.

Rational thinking is a process that refers to the ability to think with reason. It is the ability to draw sensible conclusions from logic, data, and facts. When making a decision, we use rational thinking to figure out how to effectively move from point A (where we stand now) to point B (the goal).

BE AWARE!

Our autonomous decisions are very important, but autonomy alone is not enough.

The impact of the social environment on our freedom of choice

Having the right to do something is not the same as having the ability to do it. We have a hidden assumption that after making a decision, the social environment we live in will allow us to execute our decision. But the social environment can create constraints that in practice will limit our freedom of choice and, in some cases, may even force us to act in opposition to our free will. Let's assume we live in a liberal democratic country where citizens act according to the social contract, and therefore, we can do whatever we want if it meets the two basic conditions: we are acting from our free will and not harming others. But is this liberal democratic rule enough to secure our basic rights? Definitely not. We will use examples to demonstrate.

Freedom of movement

Let's assume the city we live in has a non-functional police force. If I decide that I want to go for a run at night or go to a restaurant, the probability that I will be murdered, injured, or robbed is high because there are many criminals roaming the streets. Even if I have the basic freedom of movement, because of the violent environment, I will be forced to stay at home.

Let's look at big issues such as affordable housing, affordable education, and affordable healthcare.

There are countries where these three necessities are so expensive that people, even if they work hard, cannot afford them. Alternatively, there are countries with an active intervention policy that makes these necessities affordable to all their citizens. And, lastly, there are countries which believe that the sole role of government is to provide its citizens with internal and external security, and that most other issues should be left to the invisible hand of the free market.

The Main Points

Our autonomous decisions are very important, but autonomy alone is not enough. There will be people who believe the government has the responsibility to build an environment with the appropriate infrastructure that gives citizens the practical ability to execute our basic rights, such as a good police force that protects us, and affordable healthcare, housing, and education.

Their main argument will be that only in such an environment can we carry out our freedom to choose.

But there will be others who believe that the sole role of government is to provide its citizens with internal and external security, and that most other issues should be left to the invisible hand of the free market.

Final Thoughts

REMEMBER:
You won't earn prizes just
for knowing things.
You'll only be rewarded for your actions.
This book contains
valuable information-use it!

If this book has helped you
to better understand the process
of becoming financially independent,

I would greatly appreciate
your review on Amazon.

Thank you in advance.
— Jacob Nayman

Executive summary

Perfect World, Real World

Chapter 1
Making the Impossible Possible
What we need to achieve big goals

What we need to achieve big goals

Any person with ambition and a sound mind who uses the secret weapon strategies can achieve big, challenging goals — even without innate charisma, leadership abilities, a brilliant mind, or a Harvard MBA.

Chapter 2
Manipulation
The easy way to succeed

Why manipulation is the weapon of choice

First, using the weapon of manipulation is very effective. It can achieve quick results in a short time frame.

Second, it is very hard to legally prove that manipulation has occurred in the first place.

Third, even when an act of manipulation is proven, it is not usually considered a criminal act that deserves punishment.

Chapter 3
Gain Financial Independence
Three must-have abilities for success

The first ability you have to possess in order
to become financially independent is the ability
to quickly identify when the weapon of manipulation is
being used on you, and to say no.

The second ability you have to possess in order
to become financially independent is the ability
to harness people's limited resources
to support your private agenda.

The third ability you have to possess in order
to become financially independent is the ability
to build and preserve your wealth.

Chapter 4
Perfect World vs. Real World
What you see is what you get vs. deception

The perfect world

What you see is what you get — the private and public agendas are the same.

Make the world a better place — social interests will prevail over private interests.

The real world

Manipulation and deceit — the private and public agendas aren't the same.

Make your world a better place — private interests will prevail over social interests.

Chapter 5

The Secret Weapon

Make your world a better place

The secret weapon strategies:

Provide a big incentive to decision makers.

Exploit a big, real problem that exists in society and connect it to the agenda.

Explain in a logical way (cause and effect) why the solution is effective in solving the problem.

Legitimize the private agenda. Present a solution that makes the world a better place.

Present a solution with only two options, where one option is good and the other is bad

Chapter 6
The Game Changers
Five powerful tools of rhetoric

Big impact

The solution must grab our attention.

Effectiveness

We must create a logical explanation.

Justified socially

Even if a solution creates a social problem, we have to explain why using it is justified.

Uniqueness

We have to highlight the traits that exist in our solution that do not exist elsewhere.

Dichotomy

Present a solution with only two options.

Chapter 7
Play It Safe
How to avoid manipulation

The first line of defense: Before we adopt the agenda

Adopt critical thinking before you act. There are five powerful tools of rhetoric for getting our active support. We have to question and cast doubt on each of them.

The second line of defense: After we adopt the agenda

Protect yourself with the five risk management practices: knowledge, trustworthiness, diversification, control, and supervision.

Chapter 8
Generate Long-Term Income
Invest your money wisely

Having a good income is not always enough to secure your economic future: for that, you also have to build an investment portfolio that will generate long-term income.

In the financial markets, you must acquire investment knowledge. This will protect your money from immoral people and enable you to achieve your financial goals.

Chapter 9

Become Enlightened

Use the secret weapon

The secret weapon strategies give you the tools and knowledge you need to gain enlightenment on how to achieve financial independence. Compared to those who don't take advantage of them, using the strategies of the secret weapon will help you achieve your goals so you can live financially independent and free.

Chapter 10

Promote Social Agendas

Make the world a better place

The strategies of the secret weapon can also be used to effectively promote social agendas that are important to you. While promoting social agendas is not likely to make you wealthier, it can definitely make you feel happier and more complete.

Chapter 11
What You See is What You Get
Empirical evidence

When we encounter an entity that uses powerful rhetorical tools to harness active support for a certain agenda, one of the first lines of defense against possible manipulation is to check the entity's credibility. This means seeing if there is empirical evidence to support the entity's claims. Finding such empirical evidence will enable us to make decisions that serve our interests and goals.

Chapter 12
Personal Values
Discerning good from bad

Values and desires define the path we choose to walk — the goals we want to pursue.

Rational empirical thinking creates an effective method for achieving a given goal.

Moral values, expressed in our behavior toward others, are our compass for deciding how we pursue our goals.

Chapter 13

Freedom of Choice

Succeeding in the challenging social environment

Our autonomous decisions are very important, but autonomy alone is not enough. There will be people who believe the government has the responsibility to build an infrastructure to give citizens the practical ability to execute our basic rights, such as affordable healthcare, housing, and education.

But there will be others who believe that the sole role of government is to provide its citizens with internal and external security, and that most other issues should be left to the invisible hand of the free market.

Executive summary

Wealth Building Using the Rule of Thirds

Chapter 1:
Wealth Building
Generating long-term income from multiple sources

Invest your money in a way that will create
an income-generating asset.

Chapter 2:

Investor Mindset

Practice safety

Don't make hasty investment decisions.

Practice safety by diversifying your portfolio.

Use the rule of thirds.

Chapter 3:

The Trading Platform

Banks vs. stockbrokers

Low commissions for buying and selling securities and financial products are very important for your financial activity.

If the commissions at the bank are too high, consider working with a big brokerage firm instead.

The advantages of consulting with an adviser lie mainly in their access to central, sophisticated sources of important information.

Chapter 4:

Stocks & Bonds

The building blocks of wealth creation

A stock (also known as equity) is a security that represents the ownership of a fraction of a corporation.

A bond is a fixed-income instrument that represents a loan made by an investor to a borrower.

Unlike bonds, company shares have no "guaranteed return."

Chapter 5:

Play It Safe — Diversify

Get higher rewards with minimal risk

**There are two powerful tools to reduce
your portfolio risks:**

The first tool is asset allocation. The second
tool is buying indexes instead of individual stocks.

Greater risks should only be taken if the potential
return is high. If not, the risk should be avoided.

If you invest in individual stocks, you expose yourself to
high risk **without** the reward of higher returns.

Chapter 6:
Buy Index ETFs
Don't pick specific stocks

Buying ETFs on indexes enables you easily to implement the golden rule - "don't put all your eggs in one basket."

Buying ETFs on sectors or indexes diversifies your investments and considerably reduces the volatility of your portfolio.

Buying ETFs on indexes or sectors reduces your fees.

Chapter 7:

Stocks and the Economy

Cyclical and non-cyclical Trends

Cyclical or non-cyclical stocks refers to the correlation between stocks and the economy.

A cyclical trend is the short-term direction of the stock prices in a specific industry.

If we want to take advantage of market volatility, we should concentrate on short-term cyclical sector trends.

Chapter 8:

Define Your Preferences

Amount of money, time frame, and level of risk

The relationship between return and risk is a double-edged sword: to profit more, you have to be willing to take more risk.

The longer the investment horizon, the higher the level of risk you can afford to be exposed to.

When you buy ETFs traded in a foreign country, they will be also influenced by the currency volatility.

Chapter 9:

The Rule of Thirds

Asset allocation

A wise investor will do the following:
Invest one-third in stocks and bonds.
Invest one-third in real estate, commodities
and volatile sectors.
Invest one-third in money and its equivalents.

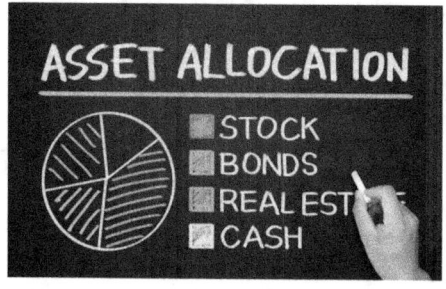

Chapter 10:

Portfolio Construction

Implementing the rule of thirds

Implementing the rule of thirds in your portfolio will enable you to minimize costs and volatility and outperform the market benchmark.

Chapter 11:

When is the Right Time to Buy?

"The best chance to deploy capital is when things are going down."

Warren Buffett

If you have the opportunity to buy securities
in a sector or an index at low prices, then increase your
exposure to this index or sector.

Implement Warren Buffet's golden rule:

"Be fearful when others are greedy.
Be greedy when others are fearful."

Chapter 12:
Rebalancing
Preserving the Rule of Thirds

Rebalancing involves periodically buying or
selling assets in a portfolio to maintain its original or
desired level of asset allocation.

In the process of rebalancing every
three months, maintain the rule of thirds.

Chapter 13:
Risk Management
An instrument that protects your money

The general premise of insurance is that you,
as a customer buy peace of mind — while the insurance
company buys your risk.

The protection afforded by insurance
coverage can be considered a risk management
tool that protects your wealth.

Chapter 14:
The Short-Term Profit Strategy
Exploiting cyclical trends

The short-term profit strategy

Buy an ETF on a sector or an index when its price drops considerably.

Sell the ETF when its price rises considerably.

Chapter 15:

Focus on Sectors or Indexes

Don't pick specific stocks

If you want to create short-term profits, investing your money in indexes and sectors using ETFs is a better strategy than investing in individual stocks.

Deliver alpha by overweighting winning sectors and underweighting losers.

Use ETFs to benefit from the positive interventions made by policy-makers.

Chapter 16:
The Value of Unknown Information
The big advantage

Paradoxically, our ability to profit as investors is increased when we buy stocks without knowing when they will rise again or what exactly will impact them.

When we buy, we assume that something good will happen in the future. We don't know what or when, and neither do the other investors in the market.

Chapter 17:
What is Moving the Markets?
Policy-makers' big impact

If the economy shows signs of an impending economic slowdown/recession, the Federal Reserve will use the QE policy to lower interest rates and positively impact stocks.

If the economy shows signs of overheating that has the potential to lead to inflation pressures, the Federal Reserve will use the QT policy to raise interest rates and negatively impact stocks.

Chapter 18:

Leading Market Indicators:

The impact on interest rates

Based on economic indicators, investors will try to figure
out if the central bank will raise, lower,
or not change the interest rate.

As long as investors assume that inflation and
interest rates are in control, they will have
a tendency to invest in risky assets.

Glossary

A

Active investor

An investor who uses his knowledge to invest money saved by underspending in a private investment portfolio. The portfolio is built in a manner that enables him to minimize costs and volatility and provides him with an opportunity to outperform the market benchmark.

Agenda

The underlying intentions or motives of a particular person or group. An agenda can be political – or business-oriented.

All or nothing strategy

The basic idea behind the "all or nothing" strategy is that the investment company takes significantly more risk than its competitors. As a result, it can produce significantly higher profits. Investors are usually not aware that to achieve these "attractive" results, the company took significant risks with their money.

Alpha returns

The alpha of an investment is the excess return of that investment relative to the return of a benchmark index.

Arbitrage

An investment strategy that requires no risk but has a positive expected profit. Formally, this means a strategy that requires no net investment; the investor cannot lose money and has a positive probability to gain profit.

Aristotle

Ancient Greek scientist and founder of the Peripatetic school of philosophy which set the groundwork for modern science.

Asset allocation

Asset allocation is the implementation of an investment strategy in an investment portfolio. The strategy attempts to balance between risk and reward by adjusting the percentage of each asset in the investment portfolio according to the customer's personal preferences, the market conditions and the economic environment. The main assumption in asset allocation is that investment in different assets results in portfolio diversification, which reduces the overall risk in the customer investment portfolio while maintaining the expected return level.

Average life of a bond

The average duration, in annual terms, of the bond. The longer the term, the riskier the bond.

B

Balancing an investment portfolio

Balancing your portfolio means buying and selling securities in a way that will return the portfolio to its desired risk levels. They do not have to be the same risk levels you chose when you first built the portfolio.

Benchmark

A benchmark is a standard against which the performance of a mutual fund or the performance of an investment manager can be measured. When evaluating the performance of any investment, it's important to compare it against an appropriate benchmark. For example, to evaluate the performance of your investment manager or your private investment portfolio you can use the S&P 500, the Dow Jones Industrial Average, or the Russell 2000 Index.

Binary options

A binary option is a financial option in which the payoff is either a defined, fixed monetary amount - or nothing at all. Binary options are used in a theoretical framework as the building block for asset pricing and financial derivatives.

Bonds

A loan you give the government or a company. When you hold bonds, you have a chance of receiving the "guaranteed return" even if the company suffers financial difficulties or bankruptcy; the company shareholders, in contrast, can lose all of their money.

Bond rating

A rating which indicates the probability that the borrower (the government / corporation) will meet their obligations and return the invested money plus the promised interest. Corporate bonds are rated according to their level of risk. The rating is given by professional companies that specialize in this area. The rating provides investors with information regarding the risk of investing in the various bonds. If the rating of a bond is low, it means that the risk - the probability that you could lose all your money - is high.

C

Capital gains

The amount of profit earned on an asset which is sold for a higher price than it was initially purchased for.

Central bank

A central bank is an institution that manages a country's currency, money supply, and interest rates, and uses monetary policy to achieve the objectives of the government. The responsibilities of the central bank include controlling and managing interest rates, setting the reserve requirement, and during times of financial crisis, helping the banking sector to function properly. In most countries, central banks also monitor and supervise financial institutions (including banks) to reduce the risk of reckless or fraudulent activities.

Charisma

A special power or personal quality some people have that impacts other people. Charisma influences people strongly and, in most cases, causes people to admire the charismatic person.

Company shares

Unlike bonds, shares have no "guaranteed return." In other words, they do not guarantee a predictable cash flow to be paid on a specified future date. When you hold shares, you rely on their market value.

Consumer Price Index

The consumer price index (CPI) measures change in the price of a market basket of consumer goods and services purchased by households. Changes in the CPI are used as measures of inflation.

Core-satellite allocation strategy

Core-satellite allocation strategy defines a "core" strategic element that comprises the most significant portion of the portfolio, and applies a dynamic "satellite" strategy to the smaller part of the portfolio. The "core" portion of the portfolio incorporates passive investments that don't require dynamic handling (i.e. index funds, exchange-traded funds (ETFs), mutual passive funds), while the "satellite" portion of the portfolio is composed of investments that demand a more dynamic approach. In the satellite portion, the portfolio is adjusted to include the assets, sectors, or individual stocks that show the most potential for gains. The expectation is that the satellite portion of the portfolio will outperform the market benchmark.

Criminal law

The part of the legal system that relates to crime, prescribing conduct that is perceived a threatening, harmful, or other endangering health, safety, property, and moral welfare. Criminal law includes the punishment and rehabilitation of those who break the law.

Cyclical stocks

Cyclical stocks and their companies are affected by the economy. When the economy shows positive signs, the price of cyclical stocks will go up. But an economic downturn will have a negative effect on their stock prices.

D

Data Mining

The process of looking for patterns and relationships in data sets to help solve business problems through data analysis. Data mining enables enterprises to make more-informed business decisions.

Decision makers

People within a company or government, who also can be referred to as policy makers, who have the power to make and execute strategic decisions that represent the goal of the entities they work for.

Dichotomy

The difference between two completely opposite ideas or things. Dichotomy in a decision-making process is when you are given only two choices, one is black and the other one white without another alternative, therefore you have only two options to choose from. When you encounter a dichotomy, it can be a true one or a false one. A false dichotomy is based on a premise that there are only two options available, while in reality, there are more.

Diversification

"Don't put all your eggs in one basket" is the golden rule. If this rule is not adhered to, there is a risk that the investments will be lost, with no higher probability of returns. Studies have shown that investing in over 20 securities can eliminate the specific risk of an investment portfolio: the only risk that will remain is the market risk. Diversification enables maximum returns with minimum risk.

Dividends

Payments made to the shareholders of a company in the form of cash or additional shares of stock.

Durable goods orders

An economic indicator that reflects the number of new orders placed with domestic manufacturers for the delivery of factory hard goods (in the near term or in the future).

E

Effectiveness

The degree to which something is successful in producing a desired result; success.

Empirical evidence

Evidence obtained through the senses, primarily observation and experimentation, documenting patterns and behavior.

Enlightened

Freed from ignorance and misinformation. Showing understanding, acting in a reasonable and positive way, and not following old-fashioned or false beliefs.

Entry premium

The difference between the price you could have paid for the stocks at the start of the rise in the Stock Market and the higher price you pay later is called the cover charge, or "entry premium."

Equilibrium

A situation where the forces of demand and supply are in balance with each other.

Equities

Another word for shares of stock in a corporation.

ETF

An ETF (exchange traded fund) is a marketable security that tracks an index, a commodity, bonds, or a basket of assets. Like a mutual fund, an ETF is a pool of investments; however, an ETF will often have lower associated costs. Unlike mutual funds, an ETF trades like a common stock on the stock exchange, and its price changes throughout the day as it is bought and sold.

Exotic financial products

Unregulated financial products that contain a lot of false promises. There are financial products that are difficult to understand, introduced as "sexy" and profitable, which are indeed composed of elements that are very profitable - but only to the seller. If you give into temptation and buy them, they can hurt the returns in your investment portfolio.

Expected return

The amount of profit or loss an investor can anticipate receiving on an investment, calculated by the odds of the occurrences of different potential outcomes.

Exposure to foreign currencies

If you buy a financial product traded in a foreign country, in most cases it will be influenced by the currency exchange of that country. Therefore, buying ETFs on overseas stock indexes, for example, exposes you to foreign currency fluctuations.

F

Federal Reserve

The central banking system of the United States of America.

Fees for securities

The level of commission for buying and selling securities and financial products is very important for your financial activity.

Fake news

False or misleading stories presented as news, spread on the internet or using other media. Fake news is usually created to influence political views and often has the aim of damaging the reputation of a person.

Financial adviser

The adviser has access to reports prepared by the economics department of the financial institution at which they are employed. These reports can provide essential information on the basis of which, among other things, it can be determined how much foreign currency you should keep in your investment portfolio, and on the basis of which an institutional recommendation can be made regarding the percent to invest in various investment channels.

Financial freedom

The ability to produce a steady income and maintain your desired lifestyle even when you don't work.

Financial independence

The status of having enough income or wealth sufficient to support himself and his family for the rest of his life without having to depend on income sources from others.

Financial instruments

Securities: bonds, stocks, and commodities

Financial platforms

A bank, an investment company, or a brokerage firm.

Financial simulators

Used to simulate asset allocations based on customer preferences while taking the macroeconomic conditions in the market into account.

Fixed income

Any type of investment, such as bonds, in which the issuer makes payments of a fixed amount on a fixed schedule.

FOMO: The fear of missing out

As investors, we can wait for the economy to heal completely, and only then invest our money in the Stock Market. However, it may take years before the economy is 100 precent healthy. And most investors won't wait due to the fear of missing out.

Forex

The Foreign Exchange global market, where currencies are traded. It is decentralized, meaning there is no central marketplace for foreign exchange; instead, currency trading is conducted electronically, "over the counter" (OTC) - all transactions between traders around the world occur via computer networks. The market is open 24 hours a day except on weekends. The foreign exchange market assists international trade and business by providing a platform for currency conversion.

Free will

The ability to choose between different possible courses of action, and to decide what to do independently of any outside force.

Future market expectations

If the market expects that the central bank will raise interest rates in the near future, the market will not "wait" until it actually happens - it will react as if the increase in interest rates has already been implemented.

Futures contract

A standardized contract that requires delivery of an asset in the future. Such contracts trade throughout the day and are listed on various exchanges.

G

GDP

The gross domestic product (GDP) is a measure of the total market value of all final goods and services produced in a period (quarterly or yearly).

Government Bonds

Always safer than corporate bonds: the government can always print more money to meet its obligations, while companies depend on their financial strength to meet their obligations.

Gravity

A force that causes objects to fall to the ground and attracts objects toward one another. Of the four fundamental interactions (strong interaction, electromagnetic force, and weak interaction), gravity is the weakest and has no influence on subatomic particles.

H

Hedge funds

A pooled investment fund that can make a large profit but involves a large risk. The fund trades in liquid assets and makes use of risk management techniques. Hedge funds are usually restricted to institutional investors, high net worth individuals, and accredited investors.

Housing starts

Housing starts reflects the number of new, privately-owned houses on which construction has been started in a given period.

I

Incentive

Anything that encourages a person to act or alter their behavior. The higher the incentive, the greater the level of effort, and therefore, the higher the level of performance.

Inefficient market

A condition to which the market values of traded securities do not reflect their true values.

Institutional funds

Investment funds that are intended for institutional investors rather than retail investors.

Insurance premiums

An insurance premium is the amount of money an individual or business pays for an insurance policy.

Interest rates

When deciding where to invest your money, you have several alternatives. The solid channel offers investments with only a very low risk; therefore, if interest rates are high, it is preferable to put most of your money in solid investments, such as government bonds.

In such circumstances your investments will enjoy high interest rates, and your level of exposure to risky assets will drop. The opposite is also true: the lower the interest rates are, the more worthwhile it is to take risks in order to generate higher returns; the level of exposure to risky assets, such as stocks, will usually be higher. When interest rates are low the demand for risky assets is higher, and the prices, accordingly, are also higher.

Investment company

An investment company is a corporation or a trust that invests the money of investors in financial securities.

Insurance premiums

An insurance premium is the amount of money an individual or business pays for an insurance policy.

Investment horizon importance

The longer the investment horizon, the higher the level of risk you can afford to be exposed to, since your investments will have plenty of time to ride out the market's short-term fluctuations. Accordingly, the potential to gain higher returns will be greater.

Investor preferences

The portfolio should be built in accordance with investor desires and needs; to accomplish this, the following issues should be addressed: the sum of money to be invested in the private portfolio, the period of the investment, and exposure to risk and the required return.

Invisible hand

A metaphor used by Adam Smith to describe the unobservable forces that control supply and demand to reach equilibrium in a free market. People who believe in the concept of the invisible hand will preach that the government shouldn't intervene in economic development if the equilibrium is not violated.

J

Joblessness claims

This report tracks how many new people filed for unemployment benefits in the previous week.

Julius Caesar

A famous roman emperor and general who was a member of the first Triumvirate and led the Roman armies in the Gallic Wars. He defeated his political rival Pompey in a civil war then declared himself dictator, which lasted until his assassination in 44 BCE.

Justification

A good or acceptable reason or explanation for an act or way of behaving. Also used by entities (people or corporations) to legitimize their operation.

L

Law

A rule or set of rules to regulate moral behavior in society, created by society or government and enforceable by social or governmental institutions.

Leading market indicators

An active government has several important economic obligations / objectives that it should actively pursue: high employment, price stability, and economic growth.

Liquidity

Liquidity refers to the portion of the portfolio that you can immediately realize to cash without incurring a loss in returns. Although you receive very low returns from the liquid portion, it's an important part of the overall investment portfolio. The liquidity allows you to act quickly if there are opportunities in the financial market. If you need a high level of liquidity, then cash and cash equivalents can meet this requirement.

Lizard mind

The lizard brain is the most primitive part of the brain; the brain stem. It is the part of a person's psyche or personality dominated by instinct or impulse rather than rational thought.

Lobbyist

Someone who lawfully tried to persuade a politician or government official to do something for the company or organization he represents, usually by face-to-face contact.

Long-term capital gains

The amount of profit realized by selling an asset held for one year or longer at a higher price than it was purchased for.

M

Manipulation

Manipulation is the use of unfair means of deception to influence, exploit, and control people's minds and, eventually, actions. A manipulator's main goal is to achieve their clandestine desires and goals, even at the expense of others. Manipulation gives the manipulated person a false sense that they are acting of their own free will. They are unaware that they are victims of manipulation.

Market benchmarks

The risky part of the investment is compared to the performance of the Stock Market and high-yield bonds, and the solid part is compared to the benchmark of solid bonds.

"Market portfolio"

A theoretical concept. It is defined as a portfolio consisting of investments that include every financial asset available in the world market. The representation of each asset in the "market portfolio" is proportional to its total presence in the world market. Because its components mirror all of the assets in the financial world, the expected return of the market portfolio should be identical to the expected return of the whole market. Since the market portfolio, by definition, is optimally diversified, it is subject only to risks that affect the whole market, and not to the risks relevant to a particular asset in the portfolio. In the process of building an investment portfolio based on the "market portfolio" concept, investors use proxies for the market portfolio such as the S&P 500 in the US, the FTSE 100 in the UK, the DAX in Germany, and more.

Market volatility

Can be expressed by inflation, deflation, fluctuations in interest rates, currencies and the Stock Market.

Mental strength

The mindset of a person that impacts individual resilience and confidence. It can predict success in sport, education, and the workplace.

Moral conflict

An ethical dilemma where a human being stands under two or more conflicting ethical requirements. The person can to one or the other, but not both.

Moral problem

A moral problem arises in any situation that involves a conflict of interest between two or more people. If there isn't a conflict of interest, there isn't a moral problem. If at least one person in the conflict sees another as only a means to an end and uses means of enforcement, deceit, or threat to get what they want, then the conflict becomes a moral problem.

Morality

A set or body of standards, both personal and/or social, derived from a philosophy, religion, or culture, to differentiate between decisions and actions that are right and decision that are wrong, or proper and improper.

Motive

The cause or reason someone does a certain action. A motive gives people the incentive to act.

Mutual funds

A pool of money from many investors used to purchase securities, which include stocks, bonds, money market instruments and similar assets. In essence, mutual funds are joint investments. When you invest your money in them, they allow you to use licensed portfolio managers to manage your investment and thereby benefit from their knowledge and experience.

Market risk of a security

The product of macroeconomic factors, such as a sharp rise in interest rates, inflation, deflation, a crisis in a major market player (Europe, the United States, or China), and more.

Marketability

The ease with which you can buy and sell securities at market price when you choose to do so.

Monetary policy

In the United States, the Federal Reserve is in charge of the monetary policy. The Federal Reserve has four main economic goals: to achieve maximum employment (close to 95 percent); to maintain stable prices (two – three percent inflation per year); to keep interest rates relatively low; and to provide banks with liquidity that enables them to operate in a "healthy" way. To achieve all four goals the Federal Reserve uses a monetary policy, which is implemented through the actions of the central bank. The main "weapon" used by the Federal Reserve is the control, and if needed, adjustment of the interest rate. It does this by financial actions such as buying or selling government bonds and changing the amount of money that banks are required to keep in their reserves. These actions have far-reaching implications for the economy, as they impact the interest rates on savings accounts, corporate bonds, student loans and mortgages.

N

Newton

An English mathematician, scientist, and philosopher. He was a key figure in the Enlightenment movement, and was one of the developers of infinitesimal calculus.

Non-cyclical stocks

Non-cyclical stocks are profitable regardless of economic trends because they produce or distribute **basic** goods and services that consumers always require.

Norms

Shared standards of acceptable behavior by groups that can be either informal understandings of members of a society or integrated into rules and laws.

Norms are an accepted standard of behavior in a given society and are powerful drivers of behavioral changes.

P

Perfect world

The perfect world is a moral utopian world without manipulations in which people are seen as intelligent entities who deserve fair treatment. It's a world in which what you see is what you get – that is, the private and public agendas are the same. Trust, transparency, and shared goals are used as powerful, effective weapons to achieve a common goal that benefits all involved parties. The main tool to motivate others to actively support private and public agendas is to connect the values, desires, and goals in the agenda to other people's values, desires, and goals.

Portfolio manager

Portfolio managers make investment decisions for a fund or group of funds under their control. They base their investment decisions on their evaluation of the financial markets. They buy and sell securities as the conditions in the Stock Market changes.

Portfolio optimization

A technique of selecting the best portfolio according to objective criteria that typically maximizes expected return and minimizes financial risk.

Presentation

A talk or demonstration that conveys information from a presenter to an audience. A presentation is meant to inform, persuade, inspire, motivate, or present a new idea.

Proactive

Self-initiated action or behavior to cause change to solve a problem before it has occurred rather than reacting to a problem after it happens.

Q

Quantitative easing (QE)

QE is a monetary policy strategy used by central banks, such as the Federal Reserve. Under QE, a central bank purchases securities in an attempt to reduce interest rates, increase the supply of money and drive more lending to consumers and businesses. The goal is to expand economic activity.

Quantitative tightening (QT)

Quantitative tightening is a contractionary monetary policy applied by a central bank to decrease the amount of liquidity within the economy. The effect of QT is increased interest rates that help to slow or keep the domestic currency from inflation.

R

Rational thinking

The ability to arrive at a systematic conclusion after considering, accessing, organizing, and analyzing relevant information guided by reason.

Real investment

Money invested in tangible and productive assets such as plant machinery and real estate, as opposed to investment in securities or other financial instruments.

Real world

The real world is an immoral world characterized by manipulation and deceit. Entities (people or corporations) see other people in society only as a means to an end: a pawn or object that should be exploited to serve their selfish goals and desires.

These entities champion public and private agendas that are not the same. Their public agenda camouflages the clandestine agenda: it pretends to serve our values and desires and to care about our well-being. But unbeknownst to most of the population, their private agenda doesn't correspond to their public agenda.

The entities use the weapon of manipulation on people to achieve their clandestine agenda that predominantly serves their desires and goals. Even worse, it's most often done at the expense of other people's personal aims and ambitions.

Rebalancing

Rebalancing involves periodically buying or selling assets in a portfolio to maintain its original or desired level of asset allocation.

Regulated financial product

A regulated financial product must meet three basic conditions:

1. It must be sold by a licensed financial entity, preferably

a financial institution (a bank, an investment company), that operates in the country you live in;

2. The money to purchase the product must remain in a bank account registered in your name, i.e. there is no demand that you transfer your money to another account; and

3. The product is simple and easy to understand.

Risk vs. return relationship

Higher returns on investments - higher profits - require more risk.

Rhetoric

Speech intended to influence people and effect behavior. It can be called the art of persuasion. Rhetoric is also used as a powerful tool to promote personal and public agendas.

Risk averse

An investor who prefers less risky investments to those with more risks. The degree of risk aversion is determined by the willingness or unwillingness of an investor to take risks in the past.

Risk vs. return relationship

Higher returns on investments – higher profits – require more risk.

S

Satellite portion of an investment portfolio

The dynamic element - the satellite portion will be built from actively managed investments. These are investments that do not reflect the "market portfolio."

The goal: The expected returns should outperform the returns of the "market portfolio."

Scientific thinking

Scientific thinking can be used as a tool to clarify the most effective way to carry out a goal. To decide how to move from point A to point B and achieve our values and desires, we will use rational thinking to find the most efficient and effective way. We can build and use a method based on cause and effect and validate it with empirical data. This method is objective and relevant to all people, no matter their values and beliefs.

Secular trend

A secular trend is a long-term trend that indicates that a particular sector of the economy is changing.

Sharpe ratio

The Sharpe ratio is a tool for the calculation of risk-adjusted return. The Sharpe ratio can help explain whether a portfolio or investment company that has returns in excess of the benchmark is backed by smart investment decisions or is the result of taking too much risk. A higher Sharpe ratio indicates better performance of the investment manager.

Social contract

An agreement in a given society between the members about the rights and duties of each. Sometimes it concerns the legitimacy of the authority of the state over the individual. Social contract arguments typically are that individuals have consented to surrender some of their freedoms and submit to the authority of the ruler in exchange for protection of the remaining rights.

Specific security risk

Derives from specific negative events such as strikes, mismanagement, embezzlement, or risk that decreases the company's profit due to an unexpected event. This type of risk may lead to a sharp drop in the price of the company's shares.

Spot market

The place where currencies are bought and sold according to the current price. The current price is a reflection of many variables. The forwards and the futures markets are used by international corporations to protect themselves against future fluctuations in exchange rates.

Spot market

The place where currencies are bought and sold according to the current price. The current price is a reflection of many variables. The forwards and the futures markets are used by international corporations to protect themselves against future fluctuations in exchange rates.

Solid bonds

All of the bonds in the solid investment part of the portfolio should meet two criteria: first, the bonds should have an average maturity of up to five years or less. Second, the corporate bonds should have high ratings (AA or higher). Bonds that do not meet those criteria are not considered solid investments.

Standard deviation

A number that measures the amount of variation of a value from the average value for the group. A low standard deviation indicates a value close to the mean, and a high standard deviation indicates a value far from the mean.

Structured product

Also known as a market-linked investment, a structured product is created through a process of financial engineering. It is a pre-packaged investment strategy based on a combination of underlying factors such as shares, bonds, indexes or commodities with derivatives (like options, forwards, and swaps).

T

Ticker symbol

Each stock traded on the U.S. stock exchange is associated with a ticker symbol. The ticker consists of a number of letters that are usually reminiscent of the name of the company that issued the shares. The ticker is used by investors in any case in which it is necessary to specify the specific stock,

Transparency

The investment company that sells the financial product is required by law to publish a prospectus before beginning its operations. A prospectus is a document that contains important details for investors, such as specifics regarding investment policies.

U

Ultimatum tactic

"I've been given an offer by your competitor. If you can't match it or better, I will transfer my money to him."

Unique

One of a kind, or unlike anything else. The only one of its type. Unusual or special in some way.

USSF

The branch of the United States military that deals with space service. The Space Force is a part of the Department of the Air Force.

Utopian

Describing an imaginary community or society in which everyone treats each other in a moral way. The members of the society possess high moral qualities.

V

Validity of an argument

The vegetarian's lioness:

Premise A: All lions are vegetarians.

Premise B: The dog that I own is a lion.

Conclusion: My dog is a vegetarian.

From the example we can see that all the arguments are false. But if somebody adopts the two (false) arguments as true and doesn't question their credibility by using empirical observation, then they must also accept the (false) conclusion as true. This is called the validity of an argument

Values

Individual beliefs that motivate people to act one way or another, and the principles that help a person decide what is right and wrong. Values serve as a guide for human behavior. People tend to believe the values of their culture are "right," and are predisposed to adopt the values they were raised with.

Intellectually autonomy – the ability and willingness to think for oneself; not being overly dependent on other when it comes to forming one's beliefs. When a person possesses intellectually autonomy he is not influenced easily by other opinions or ideas. He forms his own opinions.

VIX

The CBOE Volatility Index, known by its ticker symbol VIX, is a popular measure of the Stock Market's expectation of volatility implied by S&P 500 index options. It is calculated and published on a real-time basis by the Chicago Board Options Exchange

(CBOE), and is commonly referred to as the "fear index" or the "fear gauge."

Volatility

Likely to change, especially to become worse, suddenly. In a financial instrument, volatility is a measure of risk.

W

Well-being

The state of feeling happy. It refers to the quality of life that a person feels intrinsically.

Y

Yield to maturity

The annual return of the investor, if the bond is held until its maturity.

Z

Zero sum game

An economic concept according to which one investor's gains must be balanced by another investor's losses.